ges To Reading

OND EDITION

Understanding Reading Problems: Does Your Child Have One?

Schwab
Foundation
for Learning

A Note To Our Readers:

Educational and medical specialists use a variety of terms to refer to reading problems. The more commonly used terms—**dyslexia**, **reading differences** and **reading problems**—are used interchangeably throughout the **Bridges To Reading** series.

In fairness to both genders, we alternate the use of "he" and "she" among the books.

Printed on recycled paper in the United States of America

www.schwablearning.org for more information on learning differences

Contents

"If people knew
how hard I worked
to get my mastery,
it wouldn't seem
so wonderful
after all."
—Michelangelo

What Is Dyslexia?

Many children seem to have no trouble at all learning to read. Even when very young, they begin making connections between letters and sounds, sounds and words, words and thoughts. For these children, the process of reading seems simple and natural. For other children, however, learning to read is a continuous struggle.

Difficulties with basic reading and language skills are the most common of all learning disabilities, affecting up to 80 percent of people who have learning problems. According to the National Institutes of Health, one out of every ten children has significant problems with reading skills. Medical and education specialists use many terms to refer to these problems, including: **reading differences, reading disorders, reading difficulties** and **dyslexia.** In *Bridges To Reading*, we use these terms interchangeably.

**Learning disabilities
affect 15% of
the population.**

—**National Institutes of Health**

Dyslexia is a lifelong condition that affects people all over the world, no matter what language they speak. It is found in both boys and girls, and is often inherited, so it may affect more than one member of a family.

Dyslexia is an "invisible" learning disability—you can't see it when you look at a child, or hear it when you talk to him. As a result, many children with reading difficulties never know why they have learning problems, and never get the help they need.

Reading problems have nothing to do with intelligence. All children can learn!

Recognizing dyslexia is often made even more difficult because specific reading problems vary so much from child to child. Sometimes there are no obvious clues that your child will have reading difficulties. She may have a good speaking vocabulary, play well with friends, and appear to be ready for school. On the other hand, she may be poor at rhyming, slow to talk, or have trouble finding the "right" word when she's speaking or writing.

Whatever her strengths or needs, dyslexia will make it difficult for her to learn to read. With appropriate assessment and corrective actions, however, most children with reading differences can learn to read.

A child is considered to have dyslexia if he or she has difficulty learning to read despite having adequate intelligence, attention, motivation and exposure to education.

What Causes Dyslexia?

We don't really know what causes dyslexia, even though many experts have tried to find the source of the problem. Research has shown that some dyslexics may have a slight difference in brain structure and function in the areas connected with language and learning. Current techniques which allow scientists to actually watch the brain at work are giving us new clues about the causes of dyslexia.

Children with dyslexia show strength in many areas, but they cannot figure out the alphabetic code as most children do.

One of the things we are learning is that the brain processes the written word one sound at a time. The individual sounds that make up larger words are called "phonemes." Phonemes for the word "big," for example would be **buh**, **ih** and **guh**; phonemes for the word "cat" would be **kuh**, **aah** and **tuh**.

Once the brain learns to recognize phonemes, it can put the sounds of the letters together to decode the written word. Normal readers can do this very rapidly. Dyslexics, however, have trouble decoding the individual pieces of a written word. The brain does not process the word as quickly or efficiently as it should. As a result, the dyslexic reader cannot apply his or her intelligence or knowledge of vocabulary to get the meaning of the word.

Research suggests that some dyslexics may also have a reduced ability to rapidly process speech. Here again, the brain has trouble breaking down combinations of sounds so that they can be processed and decoded to find the meaning in the words.

Children with Dyslexia

Although they come from diverse backgrounds, children with dyslexia share one thing in common: They have trouble learning to read.

Like most eager students, they come to kindergarten ready and willing to learn. Even though they may have attended preschools and enjoy playing with friends, they have trouble learning their ABCs. They hum the "alphabet song" with their classmates, but may never get the sequence of the letters right. They are unable to connect the letters with their related sounds and have trouble memorizing basic sight words like **come**, **said**, **what**, **was** and **the**.

Reading difficulties range from mild to severe. Children with a mild form of dyslexia may figure out a system for reading words, but continue to spell poorly. Those with severe reading problems may pick up only a few alphabetic cues or sounds to assist them in reading. The child who cannot learn any common sight words in first grade, or who continues to read below grade level in second grade, may be considered to have reading difficulties.

Children are unique individuals who learn differently from one another.

A child who struggles with reading may also have problems in other areas. Some children with dyslexia adjust very well socially; others lack confidence and have difficulty relating to people. Some of these problems, which stem from an inability to grasp language, may go beyond the written page. For example, a child with dyslexia may misunderstand sarcasm and humor, or misread nonverbal cues such as facial expressions and gestures. These misunderstandings often result in social difficulties and inappropriate behavior. (See *Step 5: Building Self-Esteem and Dealing with Problems.*)

Children are unique individuals who learn differently from one another. The key to moving your child along the learning path is to understand his particular difficulties and strengths and manage them correctly. Children with reading problems are often highly intelligent.

If you can discover the ways your child learns best, you can help him make the most of his natural abilities.

They may possess leadership skills, or excel in music, art or sports. If you can discover the ways your child learns best, you can help him make the most of his natural abilities.

You can also support your child by learning about reading differences, understanding the educational system, and figuring out effective learning strategies. The *Bridges To Reading* series will help you identify some common signs and symptoms of dyslexia, find out about testing and evaluation, get help from your child's school, find outside resources, and learn to work with your child's strengths.

Identifying Dyslexia in Your Child

A child with dyslexia may exhibit many different kinds of problems, both at home and at school. Besides reading, dyslexia may also affect a number of other functions, including speech, reasoning, math comprehension, handwriting, social skills and learning motivation. These lists will help you identify some of the warning signs that indicate a child is having reading problems.

Common Signs of Dyslexia in Preschool

- Speaks later than most children

- Has pronunciation problems

- Exhibits slow vocabulary growth; is often unable to find the "right" word when speaking or writing

- Has difficulty rhyming words

- Has trouble learning numbers, alphabet, days of the week, colors, shapes

- Is extremely restless and easily distracted

- Has trouble interacting with peers

- Has difficulty following directions or routines
- Is slow to develop fine motor skills, such as holding a pencil or manipulating small objects

Common Signs of Dyslexia in Grades K–4
- Is slow to learn the connection between letters and sounds
- Confuses basic sight-reading words such as "run," "eat" and "want"
- Makes consistent reading and spelling errors including letter reversals (b/d), inversions (m/w) transpositions (felt/left), and substitutions (house/home)
- Is slow to remember facts
- Is slow to master new skills
- Relies heavily on memorization
- Is impulsive; has difficulty planning
- Has an unstable pencil grip
- Has trouble learning about time
- Has poor coordination; is unaware of physical surroundings or prone to accidents

Common Signs of Dyslexia in Grades 5–8
- Reverses letter sequences (soiled/solid; past/pats)
- Is slow to learn prefixes, suffixes, root words and other spelling strategies
- Avoids reading out loud
- Has trouble with word problems
- Has difficulty with handwriting
- Has an awkward, fist-like or tight pencil grip

- Avoids writing compositions

- Recalls facts slowly or poorly

- Has difficulty making friends

- Misunderstands body language and facial expressions

Common Signs of Dyslexia in High School Students and Young Adults

- Continues to spell incorrectly; frequently spells the same word differently in a single piece of writing

- Avoids reading and writing tasks

- Has trouble summarizing information

- Has trouble with open-ended questions on tests

- Has weak memory skills

- Has difficulty adjusting to new settings

- Works slowly

- Has a poor grasp of abstract concepts

- Either pays too little attention to details or focuses on them too much

- Misreads information

Most people will, from time to time, see one or more of these warning signs in their children. This is normal and does not necessarily indicate dyslexia. If, however, you see several of these characteristics over a long period of time, consider the possibility of a reading disability.

Other Symptoms of Dyslexia and Related Learning Differences

While many students with dyslexia have problems only in the area of written language, others may have additional learning differences.

For some children with dyslexia, the language of mathematics can be a particular problem. They may have trouble learning concepts, or dealing with math symbols such as **=**, **+**, **-**, **x** and **/**. Even if concepts are understood, a student with dyslexia may transpose the sequences of numbers—writing 23 as 32, for instance, or 209 as 290. The result may be a wrong answer that does not reflect the child's level of understanding or ability.

Approximately one-third of children identified as dyslexic also exhibit symptoms of Attention Deficit/Hyperactivity Disorder (AD/HD).

In many cases, students with dyslexia have difficulty organizing their work and materials. They may work slowly and turn in work late, if at all. They may misunderstand instructions and do their work incorrectly. They may forget their homework, misplace it often, or lose it on the way to school.

Some students with dyslexia also have messy handwriting, as well as poor pencil grasp. In school, these students often have trouble taking notes or copying from the board.

Because they may take information literally, students with dyslexia frequently misunderstand humor. They may also misunderstand the use of idioms and wonder how it can "rain cats and dogs," or why someone is "like a bull in a china shop." They may also have poor conceptions of time (before/after) and space (left/right; up/down).

Approximately one-third of children identified as dyslexic also exhibit symptoms of Attention Deficit/Hyperactivity Disorder (AD/HD), a problem that affects concentration. (See *A Guide to Reading and AD/HD*, in this kit.) Many children with reading disabilities also have problems in auditory and visual processing.

As a parent, it is important for you to recognize your child's strengths, as well as his areas of concern.

While research suggests that most students with dyslexia do not show signs of significant social and emotional problems, some do. This is especially true of children who do not get enough support or help for their reading problems. These students may develop a poor self-image and lack self-confidence and self-esteem. Problems understanding the world around them can lead to frustrations that make it difficult for them to control their emotions. Counseling can be extremely useful for these children, but a parent's support and understanding is the first step to take in helping a child with dyslexia.

Remember that while your child may exhibit these kinds of problems with spoken and written language, he may also exhibit strong abilities in other areas. As a parent, it is important for you to recognize your child's strengths, as well as his areas of concern. Build on your child's strengths by encouraging him to pursue activities he does well and enjoys.

Strategies for Communicating with Your Child's School

If you suspect that your child is struggling with reading, discuss the problem with teachers and school officials, as well as with your child.

First, find out the kind of reading instruction your child's teacher is using in class. (See *Step 4: Helping Children Read and Learn.*) Recent research has shown that children with reading problems often need help developing an awareness of phonemes—the individual sounds that make up words. Your child's school may be able to offer additional instruction in phonics.

Check with your child's teacher to see how your child can be accommodated in class. The general education classroom is often the best place for your child to get help. Many classroom teachers are quite skilled at helping children with reading difficulties. They can make modifications and accommodations in the classroom that specifically address your child's needs. Many schools also have special reading programs, equipment and facilities that can help your child. Some have teacher-support groups and problem-solving forums to help general education teachers deal with children's learning problems.

Many classroom teachers are quite skilled at helping children with reading difficulties.

If your child needs more help than the general education classroom can provide, you can ask for additional help from the school system. (See *Step 3: Working Together with Teachers and Schools.*) Most schools have teams of teachers and specialists who develop procedures for assessment and instruction of students with reading difficulties.

Teachers alone cannot make your child succeed. You are a vital part of your child's education. Teachers generally want your input, since you know your child best. Share the information you have about your child with your child's teacher. Gather information from the resource lists that accompany this kit, and share it as well.

Strategies for Supporting Learning at Home

School isn't the only place that your child learns. Every experience he has, in school and out, contributes to his ability to learn. You can help by supporting his learning at home.

You are the most important person in your child's life. Your love, support and encouragement can help him succeed.

Emphasize the fact that your child is intelligent, and that the problems he may have in reading are not related to his ability to be successful. Here is a list of some things you can do to support his efforts.

- Have reading materials—books, magazines, newspapers, etc.—easily available in the house.

- Be creative in what you make available for your child to read. If he isn't interested in a book, perhaps he'd like to read a travel brochure. Leave the cereal box out during breakfast so he can read what's on the back. Offer him the Sunday comics, or even an advertising circular if he's interested in sports, or computers, or toys.

- Look at books with your young child. Discuss the pictures. Read to your older child and ask questions about content.

- Play rhyming games with your child. Even rhymes with pretend words can help teach children word patterns.

- Play board games and word games with your child.

- Turn everyday activities into fun learning experiences. For instance, ask your child to help you navigate on your next road trip. You could encourage him to read maps and billboards and signs as you travel, think about the direction in which you're traveling (north/south/east/west), or help you make decisions about turning left or right.

- Talk together often. Watch TV together and discuss the plot of a show, or talk about important news.

- Provide a regular time and place to do homework without distraction.

- Be aware of your child's interests and encourage participation in non-academic areas such as art, athletics, dance, mechanics, music, computers, drama and leadership groups.

Letters to School

If you think your child is having difficulty learning to read, communicate your concerns to her teacher in writing. School administrators and teachers appreciate these letters because it is difficult to catch teachers during breaks, and telephone calls or conversations at school are often rushed and do not ensure confidentiality. Letters are also the best way to make sure that your concerns are documented and acted upon by the school.

Here are some important points to remember as you begin working with your child's school:

- Be sure to discuss your concerns with your child first. Explain why you are contacting the school and help your child keep a positive attitude toward the school and her teacher.

- When you write to the school, point out specific reasons why you believe your child may have a reading disability.

- Let your tone indicate that you are not blaming the teacher and that you want to work on your child's problems with the teacher and other school personnel.

- When you meet with your child's teacher, bring a list of your child's strengths and concerns. Tell the teacher about the things your child does well and the subjects or activities she enjoys. The worksheet at the back of this book can help you collect and share your thoughts and observations.

- Ask about all the options available in assessing and supporting your child's needs. (See *Step 2: Getting Your Child Tested for Reading Problems and Understanding the Results.*)

A sample letter is shown on the next page.

LETTER FORMAT:

Today's date

Your full return address

Dear Ms. Niebanck:

My son, Patrick, has always been interested in books, particularly books on dinosaurs, trains and monsters. Recently, I've noticed that he gets very frustrated whenever he tries to read. When I ask him what the problem is, he says he can't find his place and can't remember what the last thing was that he read.

Is he having similar problems at school? Can you suggest ways that I can help him with this problem? I would appreciate any advice you have on this subject.

Please call me to discuss this. My daytime phone number is (number). Thanks for your help in this matter.

Sincerely,

Your full name

Steps to Success

There are several things you can do to help your child succeed, despite having to deal with dyslexia.

1. **Help your child understand her reading problems**

    Learn as much as you can about dyslexia and teach it to your child. Even very young children need some explanation from you about the difficulties they are having in school. It is not always easy to communicate problems you might not totally understand. However, it is important to be honest and explain to your child that she struggles with reading and probably always will. Make sure she appreciates her talents and strengths, as well as understanding her areas of need. As she gets older, work with her to become a self-advocate. She may need to work harder than many of her friends, and use different strategies, but make sure she knows that she can do it!

2. **Work with the school on an appropriate plan of action**

    Your child's teacher or the school's special education professionals can help you decide what steps to take as you begin to identify specific problems and determine ways to help. You can:

    - review previous documentation
    - arrange an initial screening and/or assessment for your child
    - make decisions about classroom placement and teaching approaches
    - review daily work

3. **Work with your child's teacher by suggesting helpful classroom strategies**

    There are many ways teachers can help your child learn better in the general education classroom. To help children with reading problems, a teacher can:

    - stand or sit near the child
    - ask for volunteers to answer questions

- call the child's name before asking a question
- avoid time pressure and competition
- reward correct responses; don't punish incorrect answers
- give older students oral, rather than written, exams
- allow the child to share a classmate's notes and assignments
- give credit for oral participation in class
- help the child organize time and materials
- allow the child to tape class lectures
- encourage the child to write about topics of particular interest

4. Help support your child at home

There are many simple and fun ways to support your child's learning skills and reading abilities at home. You can follow the strategies outlined in this book, or create new ones of your own, taking advantage of opportunities that might let you introduce or practice skills at home. Support at home is one of the most important elements of helping your child read and learn.

5. Keep up-to-date records

Compile a folder of all correspondence related to your child's learning problems. Include copies of your child's confidential school files, along with data about your child from other professionals. Collect samples of schoolwork that demonstrate your child's problems, successes and progress. Keep a contact log of discussions you have with doctors, teachers, school administrators, etc. This portfolio of information will help you review your child's progress with education professionals as your child grows.

6. Become an advocate for your child, in school and out

Remember that not all children with learning differences will qualify for special services. While the law requires that schools provide a full and appropriate education to every child, most states require that special education programs accept only those students whose achievements are significantly lower than their abilities. Take every opportunity you can to help support learning, even if your child is enrolled in a special instructional program. There are many ways for your child to succeed. Find all the options available to help your child, in school and out. (See *Step 4: Helping Children Read and Learn.*)

7. **Let your child know that he is not alone!**
   Children with dyslexia may be comforted to know that many famous people have succeeded in spite of dyslexia. All of the famous achievers on this list either have, or are suspected of having had, learning differences:

   - Scientists **Albert Einstein, Galileo** and **Louis Pasteur**
   - U.S. Presidents **Woodrow Wilson, Dwight D. Eisenhower** and **John F. Kennedy**
   - U.S. Vice President **Nelson Rockefeller**
   - U.S. Army Generals **George Westmoreland** and **George Patton**
   - Statesman **Winston Churchill**
   - Entrepreneurs **Walt Disney** and **Charles Schwab**
   - Artists **Leonardo da Vinci** and **P. Buckley Moss**
   - Authors **Agatha Christie, Hans Christian Anderson, F. Scott Fitzgerald** and **Jules Verne**
   - Athletes **Nolan Ryan, Bruce Jenner, Carl Lewis** and **Greg Louganis**
   - Musicians **Harry Belafonte, John Lennon, Mozart** and **Beethoven**
   - Inventors **Alexander Graham Bell** and **Henry Ford**
   - Actors **George C. Scott, Cher** and **Danny Glover**
   - Comedians **Robin Williams** and **Whoopi Goldberg**

   While these people may have had learning problems, they showed great talent in other areas. Most successful adults with dyslexia report that they had at least one person, often a parent or teacher, who strongly supported and encouraged them.

Frequently-Asked Questions

Q. Can my child's doctor diagnose dyslexia?

A. Some doctors diagnose dyslexia but may be unaware of specific resources and programs available to assist your child. Your doctor may be able to determine if any physical problems are affecting your child's academic achievement. Ask if your doctor has had any specific training in diagnosing learning disorders.

Your school has professionals trained to diagnose reading disabilities. Contact your child's teacher or the Director of Special Education to ask about assessing for learning disabilities. To find private practitioners who diagnose dyslexia, check in your phone book under "Learning Disabilities," or check with your county's Human Services Department.

Q. Will my child outgrow this problem?

A. Children do not outgrow dyslexia. Even with appropriate instruction, they may continue to struggle. But with the right kind of assessment and help, they can become better readers and spellers. Many children with dyslexia find their own useful strategies for dealing with reading difficulties. Some tape lectures, use computers and spellcheckers for word processing, and form or participate in study groups. Support both at school and at home can help.

Q. Are all reading problems caused by dyslexia?

A. No. Reading problems may be influenced by a variety of factors. Some children may struggle with reading because they do not attend school regularly, have changed schools frequently, or are learning English as a second language. Some children may have difficulty learning to read because they have limited comprehension abilities; others may be dealing with emotional problems. Stress within the family can also affect learning. These factors all need to be considered in order to diagnose dyslexia.

Resources

Overviews & Fact Sheets

Early Warning Signs of Learning Disabilities: Basic Information about Learning Disabilities. National Center for Learning Disabilities (NCLD) 888-575-7373. Full article available at:
www.ncld.org/brochures/early_warning.html

General Information Packet on Learning Disabilities. National Center for Learning Disabilities (NCLD) 888-575-7373. Full packet available at:
www.ncld.org/brochures/geninfo.html

Learning Disabilities: Information, Strategies, Resources. Developed by the Coordinated Campaign for Learning Disabilities. To order a copy, call 1-800-GR8-MIND (1-800-478-6463).
Full text and audio recordings available at:
http://ldonline.org/ccldinfo/index.html

What is Dyslexia? The International Dyslexia Association, International OfficeMessages 800-ABCD123, Voice 410-296-0232, Fax 410-321-5069.
Full text available at:
www.interdys.org/about_dy.stm#what_is_

Other Resources

Dyslexia, by Sally Shaywitz. *Scientific American*, Nov 1996: Vol. 275, No. 5, p98-104. Full text available at:
www.sciam.com/1196issue/1196shaywitz.html

Dyslexia: A Different Kind of Mind (Video). Films for the Humanities and Sciences, 1997. Available from the publisher: P.O. Box 2053, Princeton, NJ 08543-2053. 800-257-5126
www.films.com

How Difficult Can This Be? (Video) (The FAT City Workshop) Presented by Richard D. Lavoie. PBS Videos, 1987. Available from the publisher: 1320 Braddock Place, Alexandria, VA 22314-1698. 800-344-3337
http://shop.pbs.org

Straight Talk about Reading: How Parents Can Make a Difference in the Early Years, by Susan L. Hall and Louisa C. Moats, Lincolnwood, IL: Contemporary Books, 1999.

To Read or Not to Read: Answers to all your Questions about Dyslexia, by Daphne M. Hurford, New York, NY: Scribners, 1998.

Why Reading Is Not a Natural Process, by G. Reid Lyon. *Educational Leadership*, March 1998: Vol. 55, No. 6, p14-18. Full text available at:
www.ascd.org/pubs/el/mar98/extlyon.htm

National Organizations

Council for Learning Disabilities (CLD)
P.O. Box 40303, Overland Park, KS 66204.
913-492-8755
www1.winthrop.edu/cld/
   Services to professionals who work
with learning disabled students.

Division for Learning Disabilities
Council for Exceptional Children
1920 Association Drive, Reston, VA
22091-5989.
800-328-0272
http://edap.bgsu.edu/faculty/seanj/DLD/
   Provides information about learning
disabilities to teachers and other service
providers.

International Dyslexia Association
8600 LaSalle Road, Chester Building,
Suite 382, Baltimore, MD 21286-2044.
800-ABCD123
www.interdys.org
   National, nonprofit organization dedi-
cated to the study and treatment of dyslexia.

LDOnline
www.ldonline.org
   An interactive guide to learning disabilities for parents, teachers and children,
offering both brief and in-depth information on LD and ADHD, links to resources
for different learning problems, a children's
section with games and activities, and
subject-specific bulletin for professionals
and parents.

Learning Disabilities Association
of America (LDA)
4156 Library Road, Pittsburgh, PA
15234-1349.
412-341-1515
www.ldanatl.org
   National nonprofit organization
devoted to advancing the education and
general welfare of persons with learning
disabilities.

National Center for Learning
Disabilities (NCLD)
81 Park Ave. South, Suite 1401, New York,
NY 10016.
888-575-7373
www.ncld.org
   National nonprofit organization that
raises public awareness and advocates for
legislation and services for students
with disabilities.

National Information Center for
Children and Youth with Disabilities
P.O. Box 1492, Washington, DC 20013.
800-695-0285
www.nichcy.org
   National information and referral
center that provides information on disabilities and disability-related issues for families, educators and other professionals.

National Institute of Child Health and
Human Development (NICHD)
National Institutes of Health (NIH)
Building 31, Room 2A32, 31 Center Drive
MSC 2425, Bethesda, MD 20892-2425.
301-496-5133
www.nih.gov/nichd
   Reviews of literature and information
related to NICHD research.

Further Resources for Scientific and Educational Literature

Educational Resources Information Center (ERIC)
ERIC Clearinghouse on Disabilities and Gifted Education
1920 Association Drive, Reston, VA 22091.
800-328-0272
www.cec.sped.org/ericec.htm
    National information system and resource center on education with a large database of education materials.

MedlinePlus
National Library of Medicine
8600 Rockville Pike, Bethesda, MD 20894
888-FIND-NLM
www.nlm.nih.gov/medlineplus/
    Users may search for abstracts of scientific and medical research through this free service from the National Library of Medicine.

To obtain resources listed, or to find updated resources, visit the Schwab Foundation for Learning web site: **www.schwablearning.org**

Parent-Support Worksheet

Understanding Your Child

You know your child best and have an important role to play in providing crucial information based on day-to-day experiences and observations. In order to help most effectively, it is important that you understand your child's strengths and needs, and keep up-to-date records. The professionals who work with your child rely on you to give them as much information as possible.

    This worksheet will help you keep track of your thoughts and observations, and record strategies and their results.

Parent-Support Worksheet

Child's Name _____

Describe your child's strengths

_____

_____

_____

_____

Describe your child's areas of concern

_____

_____

_____

_____

What activities motivate your child?

_____

_____

_____

_____

What activities are especially challenging for your child?

_____

_____

_____

_____

What learning strategies have you tried that were most successful?

_____

_____

_____

_____

What learning strategies have you tried that were least successful?

_____

_____

_____

_____

Which professionals have you spoken with regarding your child's reading differences? (Include teachers, school administrators, resource specialists, tutors and physicians.) What did they say about how your child learns?

_____

_____

_____

_____

How are your experiences and observations of your child similar or different from what the professionals have told you?

_____

_____

_____

_____

2

Getting Your Child Tested for Reading Problems and Understanding the Results

Schwab
Foundation
for Learning

A Note To Our Readers:

Educational and medical specialists use a variety of terms to refer to reading problems. The more commonly used terms—**dyslexia, reading differences** and **reading problems**—are used interchangeably throughout the **Bridges To Reading** series.

In fairness to both genders, we alternate the use of "he" and "she" among the books.

Printed on recycled paper in the United States of America

Contents

"For me the toughest thing about dyslexia was learning how to spell it."
— George Burns

Why Test?

Tests are one component of assessing, or measuring, a child's skills and abilities. By identifying strengths and areas of concern, tests provide important guidelines for helping and supporting children with learning disabilities. Parents who understand testing and test results are in the best position to work with the school to help their child.

A test is a sample of behaviors and abilities. The sample can be about knowledge, personality, interests, skills or a host of other human characteristics. Psychologists with broad test training often give individual intelligence tests; certified speech therapists give tests of language development; and special education teachers give tests that measure everything from accomplishment and achievement to thinking and reasoning skills.

People who design tests select questions or actions they believe are fairly representative of what they are measuring.

Parents who understand testing and test results are in the best position to work with the school to help their child.

The information gathered from well-designed tests can be helpful in understanding a child's reading and learning problems.

Tests are used to:

- screen for problems

- establish skill levels

- determine eligibility for special education programs

- plan individual educational programs

- assess progress

- evaluate individual education programs

Although tests are an important part of assessing a child's strengths and needs, no test is perfect. The information gathered from well-designed tests, however, can be helpful in understanding a child's reading and learning problems.

When testing a child for a reading disability, it is important to remember that testing is only one element of assessment. A review of student records, interviews and direct observations also contribute to understanding a child's specific needs.

Which Test?

Several different types of tests are needed to understand a child's reading disorder and the impact it has on performance. Reading tests, for instance, can yield information that helps teachers plan ways to help a child improve reading skills. An IQ (Intelligence Quotient) test is a test of intellectual ability. It may help in understanding a child's level of general knowledge and ways of thinking. Observations by specialists working from detailed checklists focus on behavior and can provide an understanding of how a child approaches learning.

It is important to get an in-depth assessment of your child's processing abilities in several areas, which may require that she take more than one test.

Tests are designed to be given either to groups of students or to individuals. One advantage of an individual test is that the tester can watch the child and notice if he is confused, tired, not motivated or unable to read.

When you suspect that your child has a reading disorder, it is important to get an in-depth assessment of her processing abilities in several areas, which may require that she take more than one test.

You should ask about the tests your child has been given and about tests she will be given in the future.

Some of the questions you might ask include:

- What is the purpose of this test?

- How can the information from this test be used to help my child?

- When will the test be given and by whom?

- When will I be given the results of testing, and will the results be explained to me?

Different Types of Tests

Three types of tests are most commonly used to assess students in school: tests of achievement, ability and behavior.

Achievement Tests

Achievement tests measure your child's skills in subjects such as arithmetic, written language, social science, science and reading. There are four general types of achievement tests:

Teacher-made or **textbook** tests are designed to measure achievement in the skills studied in the classroom. One example is a test given at the end of a chapter in a book, which measures a student's memory of the facts presented in that chapter.

Criterion-referenced tests measure levels of skill to determine the appropriate next step or level to learn. For example, a group of arithmetic problems that get progressively more difficult can identify the limits of a student's current progress and show the child's next appropriate learning step.

Diagnostic tests, which examine many parts of a skill, can help determine a child's specific problems. One example of this type of test is a reading test that includes oral reading, word lists, word attack and auditory skills.

Norm-referenced tests allow for the comparison of one student to others of the same age or grade. One example is a group achievement test, which is given to all the students in a class at the beginning of the year in order to tell the grade level of each child's skills.

Ability and Intelligence (IQ) Tests

Ability and intelligence (IQ) tests measure a child's intellectual (also referred to as "cognitive") skills and knowledge of information learned both in and out of school. These tests may evaluate a child's ability to solve puzzles, use words, follow directions, remember numbers, or copy designs. The scores on these tests are sometimes used to predict how well a child will do in school. They may also be used to help understand how the child thinks and uses knowledge.

Individual intelligence tests are usually given by psychologists to determine strengths and areas of concern and to predict a child's potential for learning. Group tests are also used to predict potential learning,

If your child has had different language, economic, social or cultural experiences than the children for whom a test was designed, test content and scores may be inaccurate or inappropriate.

but may not reflect the specific strengths and needs of an individual child. If a child taking this type of test has a reading problem, for example, and if reading is required on the test, his score is likely to be low and inaccurate.

If your child has had different language, economic, social or cultural experiences than the children for whom a test was designed, test content and scores may also be inaccurate or inappropriate. For this reason, legal restrictions limit the use of intelligence tests for children in some ethnic and language groups.

Behavior Evaluation

Behavior evaluations are done with interviews, checklists, work samples, and observations of behavior, attitudes, interests and beliefs. These evaluations are designed to help educators understand a child by measuring or describing how the child acts in different situations.

Becoming Familiar with Common Tests

School personnel often use shortened versions of test names when they talk about particular tests. The list at right will help you become familiar with the tests they may be referring to, and give you some information about what the tests were designed to assess.

Short Name	Full Name	Measures
Stanford-Binet	Stanford-Binet Intelligence Scale	Intelligence/Ability
WISC-III	Wechsler Intelligence Scale for Children, Third Edition	Intelligence/Ability
WIAT	Wechsler Individual Achievement Test	Achievement: Reading, math, written language
Brigance	Brigance Diagnostic Inventories	Achievement: Reading, writing, spelling, math, language, motor skills
WRAT	Wide Range Achievement Test	Achievement: Reading, spelling, math
Woodcock-Johnson	Woodcock-Johnson Psycho-Educational Battery	Thinking and achievement: Reading, spelling, math
Bender-Gestalt	Bender Visual Motor Gestalt Test	Eye and hand integration

The Mysterious Language of Testing

You may not be familiar with the language that teachers, administrators, psychologists and other school personnel use when they talk about tests. Here are some definitions of common terms that can help you understand the specialized language of testing.

Remember that you have the right to refuse testing, although the school may use due process to test your child.

Assessment; Evaluation

Testing is one component of assessment, or evaluation, and refers to measuring your child's skills, abilities or behavior. If the school plans to assess your child, ask for an explanation of each test and how it will help your child. Remember that you have the right to refuse testing, although the school may use due process to test your child.

Chronological Age; Mental Age

Chronological age is the actual age of the child at the time of testing. It is often written to include both the year and the month. For example, 8-4 would indicate a child who is 8 years and 4 months old. The mental age reported by some tests is the estimated level of intellectual development based on the child's test score. If a child with a chronological age of 8 years, 4 months, for instance (8-4), had a mental age of 10 years, 8 months (10-8), that child would be considered to have advanced intellectual development.

Intelligence, or IQ, Score

This score is a report of a child's intellectual ability as measured on an IQ, or "Intelligence Quotient," test. A score of 85 to 115 usually represents average performance on the test.

Scores above 115 are considered above average; those below 85, below average. Roughly 68 percent of children taking intelligence tests score between 85 and 115.

Norms

A test that gives a statistical score, such as a grade-level score (grade 4.5, for example), or an IQ score (IQ 105, for example), compares your child to a larger group of children called the "norm" group. If your child has not had experiences similar to the children in the norm group, or if your child is different from the norm group, this score may not be accurate. If your child has missed school due to illness, for example, or if he is bilingual or from a different ethnic background, the norm may not be appropriate.

Reliability Score

A test's reliability score is a description of its accuracy under certain conditions. It tells how consistent the test's measurements are.

Test Error

Tests are designed to give you an estimate, or range, of function for the skill or knowledge being tested. Educators keep this in mind as they interpret test scores.

Test Battery

A test battery is a group of tests selected to measure several subjects, or a combination of skills and abilities. A battery has the advantage of giving a broad picture of the child's performance.

Validity

This is a measure of the appropriateness of a test for a particular child. For instance, if your child cannot read, a written history test will not provide a valid, or true, measurement of your child's knowledge of the subject.

> **A test battery has the advantage of giving a broad picture of the child's performance.**

Preparing for Tests and Keeping Track of Results

There is no way to practice for an assessment. However, you can help prepare your child emotionally. Tell him what to expect when he takes a test. Explain that tests are used to identify his strengths, as well as those areas where he may need some assistance, but don't put too much emphasis on the test-taking process. Do what you can to help him relax and reduce any anxiety he might have. Make sure he understands that there is no need for him to worry about his performance.

Do what you can to help your child relax and reduce any anxiety he might have.

Keeping Track of Testing and Planning

Keep a folder of your child's progress and test scores organized by date. Even if your child is not given an individual evaluation, a folder will help you follow your child's educational growth and remember how his academic performance was measured in the past. It takes a team effort to assess learning disabilities and provide appropriate assistance for a child. The team can include the teacher, other school personnel, the administrator and yourself. Your folder will help you be an informed and participating member of the team.

Use your folder to keep track of:

- dates of communications with school and other professionals

- dates, names and results of any assessment tests given

- dates of medical exams and brief statements of results

- samples of classroom work and tests

- records of plans for assistance, either from the school or with outside support groups or professionals

- notes on progress from teachers or other professionals

- letters about testing, recommendations and special assistance

If you are uncertain or curious about any test that's been given, ask for an explanation of its purpose and examples of how results can be used to help your child.

After Testing

When all testing is completed and the results have been evaluated, and when school officials have had a chance to observe your child, you should meet with the school professionals to discuss their recommendations.

Consider the school's recommendations carefully. If your child needs special services or support, first try to make arrangements to accommodate her needs in her general education classroom. The less intrusive the program, the easier it will be for your child.

The less intrusive the program, the easier it will be for your child.

If an outside program is recommended, be sure to personally visit the site, if possible, and meet the special education staff there. Remember that the school district will arrange transportation for your child to get to the services she needs.

No matter what course you decide to take, discuss the educational changes and plans with your child to ease concerns about any new situation she may face.

Understanding the Laws on Testing

If you or the school decide that your child needs assistance beyond what the general education classroom can provide, your child will need to have individual testing to determine his special education needs. The process for testing children, and the rights of children with special needs, are protected by two major federal laws: the Individuals with Disabilities Education Act (IDEA) and Section 504 of the Rehabilitation Act of 1973.

> **Any eligible child, including those with special needs, has the right to an education that is as good as any other eligible child's education.**

Together, these regulations provide guidelines for evaluation and assessment, and assure that every eligible student in the United States receives a "free and appropriate public education." This means that any eligible child, including those with special needs, has the right to an education that is as good as any other eligible child's education. If you want more information about these laws, contact your local school district.

Tests help the school assess the needs of your child. They are the basis for deciding the best ways that a school can help. They are also used to determine if your child is eligible for special education programs, which can be tailored to your child's needs. These programs, called Individual Education Programs, or IEPs, are developed and administered by the school. (For more about the IEP process, see *Step 3: Working Together with Teachers and Schools*.)

Initiating the Testing Procedure

Testing can be initiated either by the school or by the parent. Either way, it is helpful to understand and be prepared for the testing process.

What to Expect when the School Wants to Test Your Child

Many tests administered in school are routine and are given to everyone in a class. However, some children may be selected for an individual evaluation to determine whether or not they need special assistance.

If the school wants to test a child suspected of having a disability, it must request the parent's permission in writing. The school's request to you must be written in language that you understand. It must state why school officials think your child should be tested, which tests they plan to use, and identify the professionals who will be involved in the process. The school must also inform you of your rights under the law.

> **If the school wants to test a child suspected of having a disability, it must request the parent's permission in writing.**

If you decide to grant the school permission to test your child, you must do so in writing. If you refuse their request, there is a procedure the school may use to override your decision. The ability of a school to override a parent's refusal to test a child varies from state to state.

What to Do when You Want the School to Test Your Child

If you want your child to be evaluated by the school, put your request in writing so that you and the school have a record of it. When you write to your child's school, try to be as clear as possible about the reasons you would like your child to be tested. For instance:

- to assess poor school performance

- to diagnose a problem

- to identify strengths and abilities

- to monitor progress

- to determine eligibility for placement

- to identify needed strategies

- to establish educational priorities

Address your request to the school's principal or Director of Special Education. If you'd like to see a sample request letter, turn to the "Letters to School" section of this book.

Parent groups can help you understand your child's difficulties and provide information on the laws and educational options related to your child's particular problem.

After you have written, the school must respond to your request within a certain amount of time, which may vary from state to state. If the school agrees with your request for an evaluation, they will initiate the assessment process. If the school refuses your request, they must give you written notice and an explanation of the refusal. The notice must also explain your right to challenge their refusal.

If you have any questions, talk to the school official who wrote the letter of refusal. Sometimes the school needs additional information in order to approve the evaluation. You may also want to talk to your child's teachers and school administrators. The school's reasons for not testing your child may convince you that your child's problems are not serious enough for testing.

If you cannot resolve an issue concerning your child's education, contact your local school district for information about the due process procedures that can guide you through the steps of settling your differences. You may also want to find out about local or regional support groups for parents of children with learning differences. Parent groups can help you understand your child's difficulties and provide information on the laws and educational options related to your child's particular problem.

What You Should Know About the Test-Planning Process

Whether you or the school initiates testing, you have the right to:

- be notified whenever special testing is planned

- request an evaluation if you think special education may be needed

- give or deny, in writing, consent to the evaluation plan

- request a re-evaluation to see if needs have changed

- have testing conducted in the language your child knows best

- review all records about your child and obtain copies of those records

- request an assessment by your local public school, even if your child is attending a private school

- request an independent educational evaluation at public expense if you are not satisfied with the school's evaluation

If test results indicate that your child's abilities are quite different from your everyday observations, ask about the score.

Once testing is initiated, take the time to find out about the test and the conditions under which it was given. If test results indicate that your child's abilities are quite different from your everyday observations, ask about the score.

Inaccurate scores can occur because of student confusion, cultural and language differences, time limitations, and errors in scoring.

Trust your judgment. Communicating and sharing concerns with the team that administers and evaluates the test is an important aspect of helping determine your child's special education needs.

Letters to School

You will probably have many face-to-face conversations with your child's teachers and other school officials. There are certain types of communications, however, that should either be initiated in writing, or confirmed in writing following a discussion. Keep a copy of all your written communications and notes on important conversations in your child's education folder.

Send a letter to the principal of your child's school, or to the Director of Special Education, to request any of the following:

- an evaluation for special services

- a copy of your child's test results

- a meeting to review your child's Individual Education Program (IEP), if appropriate (see *Step 3: Working Together with Teachers and Schools*)

- information about your child's progress

- a review of your child's cumulative and/or confidential file

Your letter should include:

- the date

- name and address of the principal or Director of Special Education

- a statement of concerns about your child's learning

- your name, address and phone number

A sample letter follows.

LETTER FORMAT:

Today's date (month, day, year)
Your full return address

Ms. Norma Leader
Director of Special Education
Local Unified School District
Address
City, State, Zip Code

Dear Ms. Leader:

I am writing to request that my daughter/son, (full name), be evaluated for special education services. I have been worried that s/he is not doing very well in school and that s/he may need some special help in order to learn. S/he is in the (grade level) grade with (current teacher's name) at (name of school).

(Describe the problem in your own words. For example: "Allison is doing well in arithmetic, but her reading problems place her at the bottom of the class. . ." or "Miguel seems to be keeping up with his reading, but is having trouble with his writing assignments. . .")

I am writing to request an assessment to see if (child's name) has a disability related to this problem and if s/he may qualify for services under either IDEA or Section 504 of the Rehabilitation Act of 1973.

I understand that I need to give written permission for assessment, and I look forward to hearing from you. Thank you for your attention to this matter. I hope to be able to work closely with you to ensure that my child's needs are met in the most effective way possible, both at school and at home.

Sincerely,

Your full name

Steps to Success

If your child has a reading difficulty, which may be an undiagnosed learning disability in the area of reading, he will probably take many tests to determine his needs and skill levels throughout his school years. The following steps will help you and your child as you go through the testing process:

1. **Keep a folder on your child's history and progress**

   As your child progresses through school, it is helpful to keep a folder of contacts, communications, test results, resources, strategies, physical examination results, assessments, and so on. You may also want to include filled-out copies of the worksheets you'll find at the end of each book in this kit. Then, as you work with your child's schools or outside professionals, you'll always be informed and up to date.

2. **Have a basic understanding of tests and testings**

   Understanding types of tests, what they are used for, and how they might help your child will give you the opportunity to participate with a school team in planning effective educational strategies. Find out the purpose of each test your child takes, and ask for explanations of the results of all testing.

3. **Ask for help—in writing**

   If you want an evaluation of your child's performance, or if you want your child to be considered for special education assistance, put the request in writing and send or deliver it to the school principal or the Director of Special Education. Keep a copy of your letter in your child's folder. A sample request letter appears in the "Letters to School" section of this book.

4. **Know your rights**

   Make sure you understand your rights. Whether you request testing or the school does, information about your rights must be

supplied to you by the school before special testing is conducted. The Director of Special Education for your school region and your state's Department of Education can provide you with information about the most recent laws on testing and special services. Copies of federal laws can be obtained by sending a written request to the Superintendent of Documents, U.S. Government Printing Office, Washington, D.C. 20402.

5. Explore your options

If special education assistance is not available, or if you feel you need more support, find out what types of community or private programs are available to you. Ask your school resource specialists, principal or Director of Special Education to recommend community resources, or look for information in the "Resources" lists in each *Bridges To Reading* book.

6. Evaluate recommendations

After testing, visit any program that is suggested, talk with your child about any change that is recommended, and make an informed decision. Don't overlook your child's general education class. You may be able to find a way to accommodate your child's needs in his regular school classroom.

7. Participate in the process

Participate with the school in developing your child's educational program, based on what you learn from evaluations. Keep in contact with teachers about your child's yearly program reviews and the evaluations that are required every three years. If you think it is needed, request a re-evaluation before the appointed time.

Frequently-Asked Questions

Q. What should I do if my child has trouble reading?

A. First, schedule a conference with your child's teacher. Find out what special assistance is being given now and what other help is available in the classroom (cross-age tutor, aide assistant, the use of tools such as computers and tape recorders, etc.) Find out what accommodations are being made to assure that your child is learning the general educational curriculum. Think about ways to help and encourage the teacher to keep in contact with you. Schedule follow-up conferences. Also, don't forget to investigate the outside professionals and support groups that may be available to you. See the resource lists at the back of each *Bridges To Reading* book for additional sources of information.

Q. How do I request special testing?

A. First, explore the help that you, the teacher and other classroom resources (e.g., school reading specialists) can give. If that is not enough, send a written letter detailing your concerns about your child's progress in school and requesting an evaluation to the school principal or the Director of Special Education. Under Federal law, the school must respond to you. If they refuse testing, find out why. If necessary, find out how to appeal their decision and how to obtain an independent educational evaluation.

Q. The school is recommending special education placement. What do I do now?

A. You can accept or refuse special education assistance or placement. There are a number of special education options that are available. As a partner in making the placement decisions, you should ask questions of the school team to ensure your full knowledge of your child's options. The law requires that the "least restrictive environment" be provided for your child. Under any circumstance, you should visit the special education teacher and the special setting before you make a decision about your child's educational program.

Resources

Articles

Assessing Children for the Presence of a Disability, by Betsy B. Waterman, Ph.D., National Information Center for Children and Youth with Disabilities (NICHCY), *News Digest,* 1994: Vol. 4, No. 1, #ND23. Available from the publisher: P.O. Box 1492, Washington, DC 20013. 800-695-0285
Full text available at:
www.nichcy.org/pubs/newsdig/nd23txt.htm

Testing for Dyslexia, International Dyslexia Association Fact Sheet. Available from the publisher: 8600 LaSalle Road, Suite 382, Chester Bldg., Baltimore, MD 21204-2044. 800-222-3123
Full text available at:
www.interdys.org/educator.stm#testing1

Understanding Educational Assessment, LD Matters, Summer 1998. Available from the Schwab Foundation for Learning, 1650 S. Amphlett Blvd. #300, San Mateo, CA 94402. 800-230-0988
Full text available at:
www.schwablearning.org/main.asp?page=1
.9.3&pubs=ld&id=1

Books

A Guide to 100 Tests for Special Education, by Carolyn Compton, Ph.D., Belmont, CA: Fearon/Janus, 1996.

Special Educator's Guide To 109 Diagnostic Tests: How To Select And Interpret Tests, Use Results In IEPs, And Remediate Specific Difficulties, by Roger Pierangelo, Ph.D. and George Giuliani, Psy.D., West Nyack, NY: Center for Applied Research in Education, 1998.

Testing: Critical Components in the Identification of Dyslexia, by Jane Fell Greene, Ed.D. and Louisa Cook Moats, Ed.D., Baltimore, MD: International Dyslexia Association. Available from the publisher: 410-296-0232.

Test Scores And What They Mean, by Howard B. Lyman, Needham Heights, MA: Allyn & Bacon, 1998.

continues on next page

Further Resources

The ERIC Clearinghouse on Assessment and Evaluation

1129 Shriver Laboratory, College of Library and Information Services, University of Maryland, College Park, MD 20742.

800-464-3742

http://ericae.net

The Educational Resources Information Center (ERIC) offers an extensive collection of practical and research-oriented articles and research reports on educational assessment, along with resources to encourage responsible test use. Features include an online test locator, links to numerous assessment and evaluation web sites, and an electronic mailing list on K-12 assessment issues.

Schwab Foundation for Learning

1650 S. Amphlett Blvd., #300, San Mateo, CA 94402.

800-230-0988

www.schwablearning.org

Foundation members have access to resource consultants, who are experts in the field of learning differences. These professionals are available for one-on-one guidance sessions in person, by phone or by e-mail. Resource consultants help members understand learning problems and assessment issues, find resources most appropriate for members' specific situations, and work with parents and schools to optimize students' outcomes.

To obtain resources listed, or to find updated resources, visit the Schwab Foundation for Learning web site: **www.schwablearning.org**

Parent-Support Worksheet

Keeping Track of Your Child's Tests and Evaluations

This worksheet will help you keep track of the tests your child takes and the results of evaluations and subsequent recommendations. Fill out this form and keep it with your child's progress folder. It will help you work with the professionals who will be testing your child and planning for your child's education.

Child's Name: _____

Date: _____   Test: _____

Tested for: _____   Tested by: _____

Results:_____

Recommendations, if any: _____

_____

Child's Name: _____

Date: _____   Test: _____

Tested for: _____   Tested by: _____

Results:_____

Recommendations, if any: _____

_____

Child's Name: _____

Date: _____   Test: _____

Tested for: _____   Tested by: _____

Results:_____

Recommendations, if any: _____

_____

Child's Name: _____

Date: _____ Test: _____

Tested for: _____ Tested by: _____

Results: _____

Recommendations, if any: _____

_____

Child's Name: _____

Date: _____ Test: _____

Tested for: _____ Tested by: _____

Results: _____

Recommendations, if any: _____

_____

Child's Name: _____

Date: _____ Test: _____

Tested for: _____ Tested by: _____

Results: _____

Recommendations, if any: _____

_____

Child's Name: _____

Date: _____ Test: _____

Tested for: _____ Tested by: _____

Results: _____

Recommendations, if any: _____

_____

Working Together with Teachers and Schools

Schwab
Foundation
for Learning

A Note To Our Readers:

Educational and medical specialists use a variety of terms to refer to reading problems. The more commonly used terms—**dyslexia**, **reading differences** and **reading problems**—are used interchangeably throughout the **Bridges To Reading** series.

In fairness to both genders, we alternate the use of "he" and "she" among the books.

♲ Printed on recycled paper in the United States of America

Schwab Foundation for Learning
1650 S. Amphlett Blvd. #300, San Mateo, California 94402

www.schwablearning.org for more information on learning differences

Contents

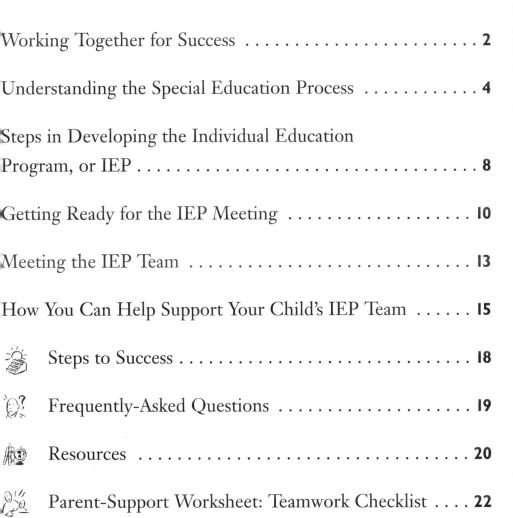

When asked to explain his genius, Thomas Edison once said, "It's 99% perspiration and 1% inspiration."

Working Together for Success

A good working relationship between parents and school professionals is important to the success of a student with dyslexia. Support both at home and at school, and cooperation between the two environments, can increase the likelihood that a child with reading differences will be successful throughout her school years.

Because many students are very different at home than they are in school, parents and educators must work as a team in planning a child's total school program. School professionals are usually open to suggestions from parents. They realize parents know more about their children than anyone else, and can be a great resource in the educational process.

In order to work as a team, parents and educators must also share goals and beliefs. You and the educators at your child's school should work together to ensure that your child receives the best education possible, in school and out.

School professionals realize parents know more about their children than anyone else, and can be a great resource in the educational process.

As an equal partner in this process, you should not be afraid to ask questions to make sure your child's needs are being met.

When discussing your child's educational goals with the school you should:

- Make sure you know your lawful rights and responsibilities, as well as the school's rights and responsibilities. Contact your local school district or your State Department of Education for copies of the laws concerning education for children with disabilities.

- Ask specific questions about how classes are taught and the methods that your child learns from best.

- Ask the teacher for suggestions regarding how your child can improve at home and in school.

- Ask about accommodations that can be provided in the general education classroom.

- Encourage the team to experiment with new ideas, and monitor and assess the results carefully.

As an equal partner in this process, you should not be afraid to ask questions to make sure your child's needs are being met.

Not all children with reading differences will require—or be eligible for—special education programs. For those who are not eligible, there are a variety of resources available. You may want to explore the possibilities of tutoring, or arrange for your child to work with her peers or with an older student. You may want to investigate the possibilities of

Not all children with reading differences will require—or be eligible for—special education programs.

your child using assistive technology, or you may be able to work with a community support group. Your child's physician may be able to refer you to appropriate resources as well. Check the resource lists at the back of each *Bridges To Reading* book for additional sources of support and information.

For those children who do require special education services, one of the biggest challenges facing parents is understanding the special education process. This book focuses on that process. It will give you information about your rights and responsibilities, and opportunities to become a valuable member of your child's special education team.

Understanding the Special Education Process

The special education process begins when a child is referred for services; it culminates with the development of a completed Individual Education Program, or IEP.

An IEP is a written document that describes a student's present level of educational performance and defines his educational objectives. It establishes goals and educational plans for children with special

An IEP is a written document that describes a student's present level of educational performance and defines his educational objectives.

learning needs, and provides an effective means for tracking progress. The format of the actual IEP document varies from district to district and state to state. If you would like to see a sample, ask your school or district for an IEP form to see exactly what is included.

```
┌─────────────────┐
│                 │
│    Referral     │
│                 │
└─────────────────┘
         │
         │
┌─────────────────┐         ┌──────────────────┐
│                 │  No LD  │  Schools are not │
│   Assessment    │╱╲╱╲╱╲╱╲╱│  required to provide │
│                 │ diagnosis│  special services │
└─────────────────┘         └──────────────────┘
         │                          │
   Diagnosed LD                     │
         │                          │
┌─────────────────┐               ╱   ╲
│                 │              │  Work  │
│      IEP        │              │ with your │
│                 │              │ child's │
└─────────────────┘              │ teacher │
         │                        ╲       ╱
    At least
   once a year
         │
┌─────────────────┐
│                 │
│      IEP        │
│    Review       │
└─────────────────┘
```

Learning together through the IEP process is one way to ensure the best possible education for a child with learning differences.

About the IEP Team

The IEP process, which is administered by the school, is a team process. The typical IEP team consists of a school administrator, the classroom teacher and the child's parents. Other individuals with special knowledge or expertise may join the IEP team at the suggestion of the parents or the school. These experts may include special education teachers, therapists, paraprofessionals or school psychologists. At the first IEP meeting, the professional who assessed your child will also be involved.

When appropriate, your child may also be involved in the team process. Older children are often included in IEP meetings. If you are considering including your child, however, talk to him, to his teachers and to other team members about his involvement at the meetings. Whether or not your child attends the IEP meetings, you should include him in the planning process at whatever level you feel is appropriate. For example, you may want to ask him what he perceives as his own strengths and areas of concern, and what he would like to improve.

Creating an Effective IEP

The IEP team must collaborate to make an effective and workable plan. Parents are equal partners with educators in this process, and share the responsibility for guiding their children. Learning together through the IEP process is one way to ensure the best possible education for a child with learning differences. With a good plan in place, students with reading problems can meet their educational goals and objectives.

The goals of the team are to:

- determine the child's strengths and needs

- determine ways to adapt the curriculum to meet the child's needs

- determine the types and amount of support necessary for successful learning

- solve problems that arise, develop new ideas, and discuss observations, developments and recent progress

- develop an IEP with both short-term and long-term goals and objectives

Identifying how the child learns best will help determine the best teaching techniques for a particular child.

In developing these goals and objectives, team members should ask themselves these questions:

What are the most important skills for the student to learn?
The answer to this question depends on which skills the family and educators feel are most critical.

How can we best teach these skills to this particular student?
Reviewing the child's daily home and classroom routines, and identifying how the child learns best, will help determine the best teaching techniques for a particular child.

Where does the student learn best?
Some educational settings are better than others. In general, the least restrictive environment that meets your child's needs will be the best for your child. Together, the team will consider where skills should be taught.

What is the best way to proceed?
Identifying goals, establishing timelines and sharing expectations will help the team plan how to best go about developing a program of individualized instruction for your child.

Steps in Developing the Individual Education Program, or IEP

There are six steps in the IEP development process. Understanding each step will help you participate in creating the best plan for your child's education.

Understanding each step in the IEP process will help you participate in creating the best plan for your child's education.

1. **Referral**

   A child aged 3 through the last year in high school may be referred for special educational services if a parent, doctor, teacher or other concerned individual suspects that the child has a learning difference. Usually, a parent or school professional initiates the process. If you suspect that your child has a reading problem, write a letter to your child's teacher and/or principal describing the specific problem and requesting assistance. Be sure to keep copies of all your correspondence.

2. **Assessment**

   Once a child is identified as struggling with learning, the school will initiate an assessment plan to determine his different abilities. (For details, see *Step 2: Getting Your Child Tested for Reading Problems and Understanding the Results.*) Your child's teacher, along with other specialists at the school, will use testing, observation and discussions with one another to evaluate his special needs. They will also review and consider any independent assessments the parent has received from outside professionals. You are a vital part of this process. Your written consent is required before assessment can begin.

3. **Determining Eligibility for Special Education**

   During testing and observation, assessment team members
   will ask the following important questions:

   - Does the suspected problem really exist?

   - Is there data to support the need for special concern?

   - Is the need acknowledged and accepted by the child's caregivers
     and others?

   - What is the nature of the problem, and how serious is it?

   - Was the assessment done in the child's native or primary language?

   - Is the child eligible for special education services?

   - Does the child require special education in order to benefit from
     the general education program?

4. **Determining Goals and Objectives**

   If a child has been determined as eligible for special
   education, a team of specialists, including the
   child's parents and teachers, devises a set of goals
   and objectives which address his areas of need.

5. **Appropriate Placement**

   Once your child's special needs have been identified,
   the next step is to determine where she will receive
   special instruction. The law states that a child with special needs must
   be placed in the least restrictive environment that can meet her needs.
   The team will consider whether your child's needs can best be met in
   the general education classroom, in a general education classroom
   with special assistance, through part-time services or by placement in
   a full-time special day class.

> **The law states that a child with special needs must be placed in the least restrictive environment that can meet her needs.**

6. Putting the IEP into Action

Once the IEP is completed, the school district is responsible for seeing that it is implemented. You should be comfortable with the results of the assessment, the educational plan determined by the IEP team, and your child's placement. Your input in this process is very important to ensure that your child meets the goals and objectives of his specialized program.

> **Your input in this process is very important to ensure that your child meets the goals and objectives of his specialized program.**

Your child's program will be reviewed at least once a year to determine how well it meets her needs. If problems arise, try to work them out with your child's IEP team members. You may request an IEP review at any time.

If you feel that your child's needs are not being properly addressed, first try to resolve the issues through informal meetings between you and the school district. If the issues remain unresolved, you can take legal action by requesting a fair hearing. District personnel can help you with this. They will tell you the information that should be included in your written request, and where you should send it. For more information on due process procedures, contact your local school district.

Getting Ready for the IEP Meeting

The IEP meeting is an opportunity for you to share your perceptions and ideas about what educational programs and processes you think would best serve your child. Preparing for the IEP meeting will help you be an effective team member and have a better understanding of how to meet your child's needs at home and at school.

These steps will help you prepare for your meeting:

1. **Confirm by mail or telephone that you will attend the meeting**
   If a conflict arises, notify the school immediately. Be sure you have an appropriate amount of free time. If necessary, arrange for childcare for other siblings so you can concentrate on the meeting without being distracted. If possible, try to coordinate with your spouse so that both of you can be present.

2. **Bring important documents to the meeting**
   Medical records, private test results and records from other schools or grade levels can help an IEP team understand your child's overall needs. Although other members of the team should also have these documents, it is a good idea to bring your own so that you can share them or refer to them as necessary. School work samples that demonstrate your child's specific problems are also helpful. Keep a folder with this information and remember to bring it to all the meetings.

If your child attends the IEP meeting, assure him that his ideas are valued and welcomed.

3. **Decide on what is most important**
   Think about two or three educational and social areas that are most important to you and your child. For instance, if a phonics program is something you feel strongly about, make sure the team understands your reasons for wanting this type of instruction for your child. If you want your child to be in a general education classroom for half of the day, be certain to mention that at the IEP meeting and in any written communications to the school.

4. **Prepare your child for the IEP process**
   If your child attends the meeting, discuss what he should expect and how he should act. Assure him that his ideas are valued and welcomed. Your child will probably feel more secure sitting next to you. You may want to show him the forms that will be filled out and

Make certain you understand everything that has been proposed for your child before signing any documents.

explain how the IEP process works before you attend a meeting together.

If your child does not attend the IEP meetings, give him as much information as is appropriate in a positive, supportive way. Make sure he knows that you believe in his abilities and are working to help him succeed.

5. **Review all documents**

    Make certain you understand everything that has been proposed for your child before signing any documents. You may take the papers home and think about them before signing. You do not have to sign any form unless you feel it represents the best program for your child, but you do need to work with your child's school to find the best program. Even after you sign the IEP form, you have the right to decide not to proceed with special education.

6. **Do not be afraid to ask for information and clarification**

    You are part of the team, and it is your right to have terms and concepts clarified, especially if you do not understand something or if things are said that concern you. Be prepared to work with other team members to make sure your child gets the best education possible.

Meeting the IEP Team

Although the people involved will vary from school to school, it will help if you understand the titles and functions of some of the educators you are likely to meet on an IEP Team. The following list outlines some typical roles of IEP team members.

Parents

- provide information on the child's talents and strengths

- attend all IEP meetings and give input

- participate in school functions

- provide support to the child at home

Child (when appropriate)

- participates in identifying strengths and areas of concern

- participates in choosing goals and objectives

Classroom Teacher

- develops class structure, curricula, discipline policy, physical layout and materials

- develops and implements instruction plans for all students in class

- works with the special educator on lessons and grading

- works with the parents and the student

Administrator

- commits resources for the services required in the IEP

- determines if the IEP conforms to school policies

- ensures that the IEP is implemented

- handles IEP logistics, such as availability of specialists, transportation issues, etc.

Assessor

- administers tests to diagnose learning disabilities
- attends initial IEP meeting and explains the assessment and results
- recommends intervention options

Special Educators

- teaches students to learn through individual or small group instruction
- helps classroom teacher with lessons, activities, tests, assignments, grading report cards and positive behavior plans
- coordinates evaluations and team meetings
- works with the parents and the student

Depending upon your child's needs, special educators with different specializations may be involved in the IEP Process. Availability of these services may vary from school to school. The special educators at your child's IEP meeting may include:

Resource specialist

Usually serves students who are in regular classes for a majority of the school day; Provides small-group remedial instruction in such areas as language arts or mathematics in a location outside the regular classroom

Itinerant teacher

Generally specializes in such areas as speech and language therapy; Travels from school to school providing direct services to students in general or special education classrooms

Special day-class teacher

Supervises the academic program of students placed in special day-class settings

How You Can Help Support Your Child's IEP Team

The success of an educational team depends upon the team members' involvement and their ability to communicate well with one another. Parents are equal partners with educators and share the responsibility of guiding their children. Get to know your child's educational support team. Introduce yourself at the beginning of the year, volunteer in the classroom, attend open houses, help coordinate an event at school, or contribute in any way you can.

Positive feedback motivates everyone. Let people know when you feel they are doing a good job, as well as when things are not going well. Keep team members informed of the progress you are making with your child and write notes about your concerns and questions. If you have new thoughts on how your child could be helped, let your team members know. Suggest a system of regular communication to address concerns and update one another on current trends and issues.

There are also a number of ways you can find help outside the school system. For example, you may be able to find support groups for parents of children with reading problems. Just knowing that others share the problems you and your child are facing can make you stronger. Often, your team members can benefit from information you collect at these organizations.

> **Positive feedback motivates everyone. Let people know when you feel they are doing a good job, as well as when things are not going well.**

Just knowing that others share the problems you and your child are facing can make you stronger.

Parents are a child's first and best continuous teachers. Working at home can help your child improve skills, and will also help support the work of the IEP team.

Here are some steps you can take to help your child:

- Discuss a homework or learning exercise with your child before he begins. Knowing what to expect will help him focus on the task at hand.

- Give your child time to look at homework materials before she begins an assignment. It is important for your child to learn how to organize materials in preparation for beginning work.

- Ask questions that have more than one right answer. Seeing many different points of view teaches your child to be open to new ideas.

  - Ask questions that require more than one- or two-word answers. Learning to give more than a "yes" or "no" answer requires your child to think her answers through.

  - Encourage your child to ask questions. Asking questions stimulates a search for answers.

- Give your child time to think about a problem so that he becomes accustomed to thinking for himself. Give him time to work on the process, as well as on the product.

- Ask your child to back up her answers with facts and evidence. By explaining how she got an answer, your child will learn to find the correct answer without guessing.

- Let your child know when an answer is wrong, but do it in a loving and supportive way. This will help him keep working until he finds the correct answer.

- Praise your child when she does well or when she takes small steps in the right direction. Your praise will help her feel good about herself. (See *Step 5: Building Self-Esteem and Dealing with Problems.*)

Steps to Success

1. **Keep the lines of communication open**

   School professionals and parents need to communicate often with one another about the child's progress through notes, letters, telephone calls or personal visits. Ask questions. Don't rush into a decision if you are unsure.

2. **Be respectful when working with other team members**

   Parents and school professionals have their own areas of expertise, perspectives, resources and points of view. It is important to respect one another even though differences of opinion may exist.

3. **Invest your time and energy**

   Take the time to understand your child's specific strengths and areas of concern so that you can describe your child to others. Trust your intuition and use common sense to effectively advocate for your child.

4. **Have high expectations**

   When teachers and parents expect the best from children with dyslexia, the children usually perform better, both socially and academically. Make sure you set attainable goals for your child, so she can succeed in her endeavors and maintain a positive self-image.

5. **Stay informed**

   Find out about the diverse resources that are available to you, both at school and in the community. Be aware of upcoming conferences and local organizations that help children with reading differences. Information is also available at libraries and on the Internet.

6. **Share your own expertise**

   You are an expert when it comes to your child. Be sure to share information about your child's developmental, medical, social and emotional history with the professionals working with him. It is also important to inform them of your child's interests, motivations, activities and hobbies.

Frequently-Asked Questions

Q. How can I help my child succeed?

A. Ask teachers for regular updates on your child's progress. Do not wait until the annual IEP meeting to find out how things are going at school. Under federal guidelines, a child with a disability is entitled to regular report cards in the same way as any other child. Ask about things you can do to help your child.

Q. Can my child get an IEP if he attends private school?

A. Private and parochial schools (K–12) are not required to provide special services to students with different needs. However, if your child is eligible for an IEP, you may want to consider having him attend private school regularly and go to a local public school to receive the special services he needs. Ask your local school district about the possibility of making such an arrangement.

Q. What does an IEP promise me?

A. An IEP outlines your child's educational goals and ways to help her reach those goals. It is a plan for special services—such as counseling, speech and language therapy, etc.—but it does not guarantee your child's progress.

Q. Which special education services can my child receive without an assessment?

A. None. In order to receive special education services, your child must be assessed (tested for learning disabilities) and considered eligible for special services under federal guidelines. Only then can appropriate services be identified and written into an IEP plan.

Resources

Articles

Collaboration between Home and School, Q&A, *LD Matters*, Fall 1999. Available from the Schwab Foundation for Learning, 1650 S. Amphlett Blvd. #300, San Mateo, CA 94402. 800-230-0988
Full text available at:
www.schwablearning.org

A Primer on IDEA 1997 and Its Regulations, *CEC Today*, Newsletter of The Council for Exceptional Children April/May 1999: Vol. 5, No. 7.
Full text available at:
www.ldonline. org/ld_indepth/special_education/cec_idea_primer.html

General Resources

Better IEPs: How to Develop Legally Correct and Educationally Useful Programs, by Barbara D. Bateman and Mary Anne Linden, Longmont, CO: Sopris West, Inc., 1998.

The Complete IEP Guide: How to Advocate for Your Special Ed Child, by Lawrence M. Siegel and Marcia Stewart (Editor), Berkeley, CA: Nolo Press, 1999.

Finding Help When Your Child Is Struggling in School, by Lawrence J. Greene, New York, NY: Golden Books, 1998.

Getting the Best Education for Your Child: A Parent's Checklist, by James Keogh, New York, NY: Random House, 1997.

Meeting with Success: Ten Tips for a Successful I.E.P. (Video). Waltham, MA: Learning Disabilities Association of Massachusetts. Available from the publisher: 1275 Main Street, Waltham, MA 02451.
781-891-5009
www.ldanatl.org/Massachusetts/projects.htm

Negotiating the Special Education Maze: A Guide for Parents & Teachers by Winifred Anderson, Stephen Chitwood (Contributor), Deidre Hayden (Contributor), Bethesda, MD: Woodbine House, Inc., 1997.

Parents' Complete Special-Education Guide: Tips, Techniques, and Materials for Helping Your Child Succeed in School and Life, by Roger Pierangelo, Ph.D., and Robert Jacoby, West Nyack, NY: Center for Applied Research in Education, 1996.

Internet Resources

The United States Department of Education Office of Special Education and Rehabilitative Services (OSERS)

IDEA 97: Individuals with Disabilities Education Act 1997 Amendments and Related Information.
www.ed.gov/offices/OSERS/IDEA/regs.html

LDOnline

Legal and Legislative Issues
www.ldonline.org/ld_indepth/legal_legislative/legal_legislative.html

Organizations

Council of Parent Attorneys and Advocates (COPAA),
P.O. Box 81-7327, Hollywood, FL 33081-0327
954-966-4489
www.copaa.net

COPAA is an independent, nonprofit organization of attorneys, advocates and parents established to improve the quality and quantity of legal assistance for parents of children with disabilities.

National Center for Law and Learning Disabilities (NCLLD),
P.O. Box 368, Cabin John, MD 20818.
301-469-8308

NCLLD is a non-profit organization that provides education, advocacy, analysis of legal issues, policy recommendations and resource materials.

National Association of Protection and Advocacy Systems,

900 Second Street, NE, Suite 211, Washington, DC 20002.
202-408-9514
www.protectionandadvocacy.com/

Provides literature on legal issues and referrals to federally-mandated programs that advocate for the rights of people with disabilities.

Schwab Foundation for Learning

1650 S. Amphlett Blvd., #300, San Mateo, CA 94402.
800-230-0988
www.schwablearning.org

Foundation members have access to resource consultants, who are experts in the field of learning differences. These professionals are available for one-on-one guidance sessions in person, by phone or by e-mail. Resource consultants help members understand learning problems and can clarify parents' rights within the education system. In addition, they find resources most appropriate for members' specific situations, and work with parents and schools to optimize students' outcomes.

To obtain resources listed, or to find updated resources, visit the Schwab Foundation for Learning web site: **www.schwablearning.org**

Parent-Support Worksheet

Teamwork Checklist

As you work with the various professionals who will be helping your child, use the following checklist to reflect on your relationships with team members and identify any areas that need improvement.

Question	Yes	No	Undecided
1. Does open communication exist between myself and the education professionals?	☐	☐	☐
2. Do team members feel comfortable expressing feelings and ideas at meetings?	☐	☐	☐
3. Do I feel like a valued team member at the IEP meetings?	☐	☐	☐
4. Do I feel that the special education program is meeting the needs of my child?	☐	☐	☐
5. Do I feel that the general education program is meeting the needs of my child?	☐	☐	☐
6. Do I make an effort to stay informed of my child's progress?	☐	☐	☐
7. Do I correspond with the school in a timely manner?	☐	☐	☐
8. Do other team members communicate changes in my child's situation in a timely manner?	☐	☐	☐
9. Do I help support my child's learning at home?	☐	☐	☐
10. Is my child feeling positive about herself and her achievements?	☐	☐	☐

Notes

Notes

_____

_____

_____

_____

_____

_____

_____

_____

_____

_____

_____

_____

_____

_____

_____

_____

_____

_____

_____

_____

_____

_____

_____

_____

_____

_____

_____

_____

4

Helping Children Read and Learn

Schwab
Foundation
for Learning

A Note To Our Readers:

Educational and medical specialists use a variety of terms to refer to reading problems. The more commonly used terms—**dyslexia**, **reading differences** and **reading problems**—are used interchangeably throughout the **Bridges To Reading** series.

In fairness to both genders, we alternate the use of "he" and "she" among the books.

Printed on recycled paper in the United States of America

www.schwablearning.org for more information on learning differences

Contents

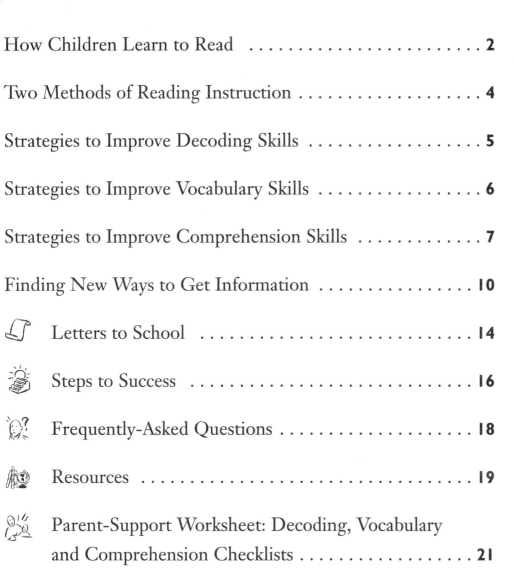

"If a man does not keep pace with his companions, perhaps it is because he hears a different drummer. Let him step to the music which he hears, however measured or far away."—Thoreau

How Children Learn to Read

In its written form, the English language is made up of 26 symbols—the letters of the alphabet—which stand for specific sounds. These sounds are the building blocks of speaking and reading. While speaking comes naturally, reading does not. It must be learned.

Studies have shown that successful readers follow these four steps when they learn to read:

1. **Children become aware that words are made up of sounds.** Children who understand that written words are made up of specific sounds, or **phonemes,** have the building blocks they need to begin reading. These children can connect letters of the alphabet to the

While speaking comes naturally, reading does not. It must be learned.

sounds the letters make, a process called **phonics.** They rhyme words easily and enjoy playing word games. Children who do not have these abilities, however, have problems learning to read.

2. **Children begin blending sounds together to make words.**
   In order to read and spell, children must be able to blend sounds together into groups of sounds, called **syllables,** and then group syllables together to make whole words. They must also be able to break down words into syllables, and syllables into individual sounds.

3. **Children begin to recognize whole words.**
   Being able to recognize written words quickly and automatically is the next step in being able to read. This process of word recognition, called **decoding,** takes practice. For children with reading difficulties, decoding words quickly and fluidly takes much more practice, but can be learned.

4. **Children begin to understand what they read.**
   The ultimate goal of reading is being able to get meaning from printed words. Reading comprehension occurs only when all of the previous steps of this process are working well. For example, if decoding words is slow and laborious, the meaning is forgotten by the time the sentence is read.

A child who has problems reading may experience difficulties with any or all of these components.

Two Methods of Reading Instruction

Today, schools primarily use two different ways to teach reading: the **whole-language** method and the **phonics** method.

The whole-language method of reading emphasizes the meanings of words and sentences. It teaches children to recognize words, one by one. Children pick up the meaning of a word from its use in a sentence or paragraph.

The phonics method of reading teaches recognition of words through the use of letter-to-sound relationships. With this approach, students learn the sounds of the consonant and vowel patterns that make up words, along with the spelling rules of the English language. Students then use these patterns as strategies for reading many thousands of words.

It is important to match the teaching approach to each child's skills and abilities. Children with reading differences usually need explicit instruction in decoding words and identifying the sounds that go with each letter of the alphabet.

One successful way to do this is for a teacher to use a multisensory method—that is, by having the child learn by using many of his senses. In learning the short vowel sound of the **a** in **apple**, for example, the student might see the letter written on the board, hear the sound said out loud to him, and write the letter down as he says the word back to the teacher. The teacher might even bring in a real apple to add feel, smell and taste to the lesson. The student might draw the letter in the air with his finger, repeat it in poems and songs, find it in other words, or even **walk** the letter's shape by following a large pattern on a floor or a playground.

> **The whole-language method of reading emphasizes the meanings of words and sentences.**

> **The phonics method of reading teaches recognition of words through the use of letter-to-sound relationships.**

Multisensory instruction is systematic and sequential. It focuses on the common patterns found in English words. These patterns assist children in reading and spelling words. Children actually learn the structure of the language by learning to read using this method.

Strategies to Improve Decoding Skills

Children with reading differences generally have problems with word recognition. They may read a new word slowly or incorrectly, or have trouble understanding the word's meaning in a sentence. There is a systematic process that teachers use to help children with reading problems learn to decode words. But you can also work with your child to improve her decoding skills. These strategies can help your child become more familiar with letter sounds and patterns.

It is important to match the teaching approach to each child's skills and abilities.

1. Read to and with your child often. Have many books around and make frequent trips to the library.

2. As you read to your child, point out words that rhyme because they contain the same vowel and final consonant, such as **fat**, **mat** and **sat** or **moon**, **spoon** and **loon.**

3. Point out consistent patterns that may appear in a story, such as words ending in **-ing**, or **-er**, or words that begin with the same prefix such as **return** or **redo.**

4. Read aloud and have your child read along with you, either silently or out loud. You can read billboards or street signs together while driving in the car, or you can write down the words to a favorite song or poem and then practice reading them from the written page.

5. Help your older child find the prefixes, roots and suffixes in words like **submarine**, **photograph** and **normally**. This practice will help your child use structural analysis to decode words.

Expressive language brings vivid meaning to a child's thoughts and ideas.

Strategies to Improve Vocabulary Skills

A child's vocabulary consists of two different kinds of words, receptive words and expressive words.

Receptive vocabulary refers to the words your child **receives**—that is, the words that come in to her when she sees or hears them. Receptive vocabulary helps children understand spoken or written information, follow directions, and link objects or events to particular words.

Expressive vocabulary refers to the words your child uses to **express** himself—that is, the words that he uses when he talks to someone or writes a story. Expressive language brings vivid meaning to a child's thoughts and ideas. As your child's expressive vocabulary improves, he becomes more precise in the words he uses when he speaks and writes.

Here are some strategies you can use to help improve your child's vocabulary:

1. Use precise words when you label objects, people or places. Say, for instance, "Uncle Joe is about three inches taller than Aunt Inez."

2. Ask your child precise questions, such as, "What did you and Tommy eat when you went out to dinner with his parents?" Wait for your child to answer.

3. As you introduce new words, use them in several settings and contexts. For example, if you tell your child about a big oak tree you climbed when you were a child, point out an oak to him the next time you see one, or show him a picture of an oak in a gardening book.

4. When you read with your child, point out clues to the meanings of words found in the rest of the sentence. For example, if you read the word **skiff**, help your child find the clues in the story that could help him figure out that a skiff is a kind of boat. Using context clues will be helpful for the child's independent reading.

5. Point out the structural clues to the meanings of words found in their prefixes, roots and suffixes. For example, contrast the meaning of the words **dislike** and **unlike**, or discuss the structural clues found in the words **report**, **export** and **deport**.

Strategies to Improve Comprehension Skills

Your child's comprehension or understanding of written words depends on these three skills:

- the ability to recognize single words

- the ability to develop a vocabulary appropriate to her age

- the ability to read fluently

To understand what she reads, a reader must know how the parts of the sentence work together.

Your child must also understand the meaning of the words in a sentence and, as she progresses, the meaning of words in a paragraph, page and story.

To understand what she reads, a reader must know how the parts of the sentence work together. For example, a young child who reads **Jack fell down and broke his crown** should be able to find the subject (Jack) and the verb (fell), which tells what is happening and who it is happening to. The older child should be able to find out—or figure out—the exact meaning of the word **crown** (head), and realize that the pronoun **his** refers back to Jack.

Talk to your child about different kinds of writing styles, including humor, dialogue, fantasy, etc.

To understand a paragraph, a reader must comprehend the topic of the story, the main idea of the paragraph, and supporting details. In longer written works, such as a short story, the reader must also understand the functions of the opening and closing paragraphs. If older students can identify the style of a paragraph—descriptive (giving specific details), sequential (putting information in order), or argumentative/persuasive (convincing the reader of what is happening)—they will have a better understanding of the text.

Written text can be separated into two forms: narrative and expository. Narrative texts are stories that contain basic elements of character, setting and plot. Expository texts are found in factual writing, such as social studies or science text books. As your child gets older, he must be able to understand the difference between these styles, and recognize other styles, such as the persuasive writing styles found in newspaper editorials or advertising copy, which try to influence the way a reader thinks. Recognizing these forms will strengthen your child's comprehension skills.

These strategies can help your child improve his comprehension skills:

1. As appropriate to your child's age, discuss the elements of a story as you read together. Ask her to name the main characters and summarize the plot. Talk about different kinds of writing styles, including humor, dialogue, fantasy, etc.

TIMELINE (story: Cinderella)				
1. Cinderella lives with her mean stepmother and stepsisters.	**2.** Cinderella wants to go to the ball, but her stepmother won't let her.	**3.** The stepmother and stepsisters go to the ball and leave Cinderella home alone.	**4.** Cinderella's fairy god-mother uses magic to help Cinderella go to the ball, but tells her the magic stops at midnight.	**5.** Dressed in a be gown and glass slippers, Cinder goes to the ball

2. Discuss the story elements found in the plot of a television show or movie you watch with your child.

3. Tape important sections of a story or textbook for your child so he can hear them spoken out loud. Listen to these sections several times and discuss key points together.

4. For older children, contrast the attitudes and behaviors of several characters in a graphic organizer, such as the matrix shown below. You can make a matrix like this for a story your child knows by heart (fairy tales, movie plots) or reads in a book.

MATRIX (story: Cinderella)

Character:	Cinderella	Stepmother	Stepsister 1	Stepsister 2	Fairy Godmother	Prince
Looks:	beautiful	crabby, strict	tall, skinny	short, fat	plump, old	handsome
Clothing:	raggedy, old	new, expensive	new, expensive	new, expensive	crazy, colorful, has a wand	fancy uniform
Action:	wants to go to the ball	won't let Cinderella go to the ball	makes Cinderalla do all her work	steals all of Cinderella's food	uses magic to help Cinderella go to the ball	falls in love with Cinderella
Personality:	sweet, gentle, sad	mean, selfish	mean, picky	loud, greedy	nice, helpful, magical	nice

5. Have your child draw a timeline of important events, such as the events in her own life, or in a story she knows or is reading. The chart below, across the bottom of both pages, is one example:

	7.	8.	9.	10.
...erella dances the prince. He in love with her.	When the clock strikes midnight, Cinderella runs away so the Prince doesn't see her as she really is.	A glass slipper falls off Cinderella's foot. The prince picks it up.	The prince searches his kingdom for the girl whose foot fits the glass slipper.	The prince finds Cinderella, marries her, and they live happily ever after.

Learning a variety of these strategies will improve not only your child's reading skills, but also her writing skills. With your support, she will be able to use what she learns about text styles, organization, and the elements of sentences and paragraphs to write her own stories and reports.

Finding New Ways to Get Information

Information is power, and reading is a tool to get information. Children who cannot read well may feel powerless and ineffective, especially in school. Reading is just one way, however, to get information. Successful children—even those with serious reading problems—can learn to be good detectives. They can find information, answer questions and solve mysteries in many different ways.

Effective questioning is a critical skill for a child with reading difficulties.

Listening

Listening is more than just hearing. Listening means paying close attention to sounds and words, and noticing what is being said. Children with dyslexia need to get much of their information by listening to the teacher, to other children and to their parents. They may need to repeat important points, either verbally or silently.

Questioning

Effective questioning is a critical skill for a child with reading difficulties. The ability to ask questions—of others or of herself—can help with problem-solving at home and at school. Help your child think about the kinds of question words that can make her a good detective, such as: Who, What, Where, When, Why and How.

Visualizing

Sometimes, a child with learning difficulties has an easier time remembering information if it is presented—and then remembered—visually. Simple images can help tie words and ideas together. They can help a child understand causes and effects, remember step-by-step sequences, or identify associations and connections.

SHARK

More than 200 teeth

Large liver

5 gills on each side

CAUSE	EFFECT	RESULT

Fire destroys trees & grass	**Bare soil does not hold water well**	**Rain brings flooding**

STEP 1	STEP 2	STEP 3	STEP 4

Plant seed	**Provide water and sun**	**Harvest crop**	**Save seed**

Using technology

Some of the best ways to get information include audio, visual and physical forms of communication. Any tool that helps your child learn is a legitimate alternative to reading.

Any tool that helps your child learn is a legitimate alternative to reading.

Remembering

If you can read, you can reread and refresh your memory. This is a luxury that is not available to children with reading difficulties. For these children, a good memory can be a big help. Here are some steps you can take to help your child remember information:

For children with reading difficulties, a good memory can be a big help.

Make sure learning has taken place. Check what your child remembers immediately after learning. Ask him simple questions: "What did you just learn about?" "What was important about that?" "How did that change things?" If the answer is "I don't know," or "nothing," then ask more specific questions. "Who discovered that?" "What year was it?" "Did it work?"

Put learning to use with action! Knowledge and skills are best learned when a child explains, discusses, demonstrates or applies information. Pretend you are the student and have your child teach you what she just learned. Put new measurement skills to work by letting your child help you bake a cake. Or make believe you are the people in a history book and act out the parts together.

Think about the information. Ask your child how he feels about the information he just learned. Ask questions that will help him think about the information from different points of view: "Does it remind you of anything?" "Do you think that was a good idea?" "How would you have done it?" "What do you think happened next?"

Use the information over and over again. Review what your child learns daily. Go over recent topics before she goes to bed, or while you're driving her to school in the morning. Discuss the learned topics on a regular basis, and not just in terms of homework. For instance, "I'm going to call Aunt Marge right now. Do you want to tell her how you helped measure everything when we made brownies last night?"

Use a memory strategy. One highly effective memory strategy is known as RCRC—Read, Cover, Remember, Check. First, the child **reads** or follows along as another person reads. Then the material on the page is **covered.** The child is asked to **remember** what he just read. (Any approximation is encouraged. If the task is too difficult, read shorter passages and then discuss the content with your child.) Finally, the material is reviewed to **check** the child's understanding.

Knowledge and skills are best learned when a child explains, discusses, demonstrates or applies information.

Letters to School

If you are concerned about your child's progress in reading, start by telling his teachers about your concerns. Since teachers spend most of their time in the classroom and cannot be reached easily, a letter may be the best way to begin communicating. Here are some things you may want to discuss with the teacher:

- difficulty or length of reading and homework assignments

- different ways to measure your child's understanding of a topic

- scheduling a meeting to discuss a particular project

- getting extra help for your child's reading and writing assignments

- problems related to school such as study skills, organization, assignments and tests

This sample letter at right can help guide you if you want to request a teacher's assistance:

LETTER FORMAT:

Today's date (month, day, year)

Dear Mr. Johnson:

Terry is enjoying school and seems to be learning a lot this year. However, she sometimes becomes discouraged by her homework assignments. As you know, Terry has difficulty (describe problem), and sometimes it takes her quite a long time to read the homework instructions and complete the assignment.

Is there a way to simplify the homework instructions or to customize Terry's homework so that she can demonstrate that she is learning using less reading and writing? Instead of struggling to write out her answers, perhaps she could draw pictures to illustrate what she has learned, or could tape record her answers to questions. Please let me know if you like these ideas, or if you have other ideas about how to solve Terry's homework problem.

Thank you for your help in this matter. You can reach me at (insert your address or telephone number when you can be reached, and when). I look forward to talking with you.

Sincerely,

Your full name

Steps to Success

The following steps will guide you as you help your child with reading and learning skills.

1. **Communicate with your child, both in conversation and in writing**
   Communicating with your child can help him develop many different language skills. Talk with him, write to him, have discussions with him whenever you can. Let him read the shopping list when you go to the store, or leave notes or simple instructions for him on the refrigerator door. Talk with him about the characters, story lines and time lines in his favorite television show. Analyzing something familiar can help him make a similar analysis of a story he reads in a book. Take the time to talk to your child whenever you can. Support and attention from a parent can also boost a child's confidence and self-esteem.

2. **Help your child expand her vocabulary**
   Help your child stretch her vocabulary by introducing specific words as you talk together. If you see a flower growing by the side of the road, say "Look at the size of that daisy!" If you see someone with a dog, say "That lady has the same color hair as her cocker spaniel!" The more specific words she learns, the better she will be at communicating—both in conversation and on paper.

3. **Talk to your child's teacher**
   Ask your child's teacher what strategies are being used to teach decoding, vocabulary and comprehension skills at school, and find out what you can do to help.

4. **Help your child understand the structure of written language**
   Point out the structure of written language as you read with your child. Discussing some of the technical aspects of writing—introductory paragraphs, descriptive texts, persuasive

writing, etc.—can help her comprehension skills. A child who has difficulty with decoding may benefit by learning how to analyze single words. Word analysis strategies include learning syllable patterns, how letters and sounds correspond, and how meaning units—such as prefixes, roots and suffixes—can be put together to make complex words.

5. Experiment with new strategies

Different children learn best in different ways. If your child has trouble reading, don't hesitate to find ways to support his learning. Work with him to improve his memory and listening skills. If pictures work better than words, help him draw or visualize information. Look into different kinds of technology that can expand his learning abilities—tape recorders, hand-held spell checkers, computer programs, etc.

6. Help make your child an active learner

In addition to teaching your child to read, help him develop his listening, questioning and memory skills. Make sure he knows that reading is only one of many learning strategies. Give him the skills he needs to learn on his own, through both reading and alternative methods of getting information.

Frequently-Asked Questions

Q. Will my child learn to read using the whole-language approach?

A. Some children learn to read easily using the whole-language approach. But many whole-language programs include little or no instruction in phoneme awareness or phonics skills. Studies from the National Institutes of Health on reading instruction note that many children, even those who do not have reading disorders, have difficulty learning to decode adequately with the whole-language approach. These researchers believe that direct instruction with emphasis on phonemic awareness and the alphabet code is needed to supplement and balance whole-language instruction.

Q. What is the best method for teaching children with reading problems?

A. No single teaching method works with all chidren, so teachers must identify how each child learns best. A structured approach emphasizing seeing, hearing, touching and feeling appears to be effective for teaching decoding to many children with reading differences. Most well-balanced reading programs also include strong spelling and writing components.

Q. My daughter seems to understand information when she hears it, but not when she sees it. Why is this?

A. Children with reading difficulties often understand what they hear, but not what they read. This happens because they cannot decode important individual words as they read. Strong listening comprehension coupled with poor reading comprehension is one of the early signs of dyslexia.

Resources

ooks

eginning to Read: Thinking and earning About Print—A Summary, y Marilyn Adams, Champaign, IL: radford Books, 1994.

Games for Reading: Playful Ways to Help Your Child Read, by Peggy Kaye, New York, NY: Pantheon Books, 1984.

How to Develop Your Child's Gifts and Talents in Reading, by Martha Cheney, Los Angeles, CA: Lowell House, 1996.

Learning to Learn, by Carolyn Olivier and Rosemary F. Bowler, with an introduction by Bill Cosby, New York, NY: Fireside, 1996.

Phonics Pathways: Clear Steps to Easy Reading, 7th edition, by Dolores G. Hiskes, Livermore, CA: Dorbooks, 1996.

Phonics They Use: Words for Reading and Writing, 2nd edition, by Patricia M. Cunningham, New York, NY: Harper Collins, 1995.

Starting Out Right: A Guide to Promoting Children's Reading Success, by the National Research Council, Washington, DC: National Academy Press, 1999. Full text available at: **www.nap.edu/readingroom/books/sor/**

Straight Talk about Reading: How Parents Can Make a Difference in the Early Years, by Susan L. Hall and Louisa C. Moats, Lincolnwood, IL: Contemporary Books, 1999.

Guides to Excellent Books for Kids

99 Ways to Get Kids to Love Reading and 100 Books They'll Love, by Mary Leonhardt, New York, NY: Three Rivers Press, 1997.

Best Books for Beginning Readers, by Thomas G. Gunning, Boston, MA: Allyn & Bacon, 1997.

Beyond Words: Picture Books for Older Readers and Writers, edited by Susan Benedict and Lenore Carlisle, Portsmouth, NH: Heinemann, 1992.

The New Read-Aloud Handbook: 4th edition, by Jim Trelease, New York, NY: Penguin Books, 1989.

continues on next page

Internet Resources

Children's Literature Web Guide
www.acs.ucalgary.ca/~dkbrown/index.html

Helping Your Child Learn to Read
U.S. Department of Education
Office of Educational Research and
Improvement: **www.ed.gov/pubs/parents/
Reading/index.html**

To obtain resources listed, or to find updated resources, visit the Schwab Foundation fo
Learning web site: **www.schwablearning.org**

Parent-Support Worksheet:

Decoding, Vocabulary and Comprehension Checklists

Fill out these three checklists to determine specific areas in which your child might have reading problems—decoding, vocabulary and/or comprehension skills. Remember to keep your child's age in mind. Your child's teacher can help you determine what level of accomplishment is appropriate for each grade.

Checklist for Decoding Skills

My child:	Usually	Sometimes	Seldom
Understands the sounds within words	☐	☐	☐
Can blend sounds into words	☐	☐	☐
Can divide words into sounds	☐	☐	☐
Has an adequate sight or reading vocabulary	☐	☐	☐
Easily memorizes new words	☐	☐	☐
Reads words aloud accurately	☐	☐	☐
Reads words aloud fluently	☐	☐	☐

continues on next page

Checklist for Vocabulary Skills

My child:	Usually	Sometimes	Seldom
• Readily understands words spoken to him	☐	☐	☐
• Appears to understand the words he reads	☐	☐	☐
• Uses precise words in speaking and writing	☐	☐	☐
• Figures out word meanings from context	☐	☐	☐
• Can analyze the structure of a word to understand its meaning	☐	☐	☐

Checklist for Comprehension Skills

My child:	Usually	Sometimes	Seldom
• Understands the precise meanings of words	☐	☐	☐
• Understands the main idea in a paragraph	☐	☐	☐
• Can read several paragraphs and summarize them accurately	☐	☐	☐
• Understands the elements of a story	☐	☐	☐
• Can graphically organize a story or summarize a passage	☐	☐	☐

Notes

Notes

5

Building Self-Esteem and Handling Problems

Schwab
Foundation
for Learning

A Note To Our Readers:

Educational and medical specialists use a variety of terms to refer to reading problems. The more commonly used terms—**dyslexia**, **reading differences** and **reading problems**—are used interchangeably throughout the **Bridges To Reading** series.

In fairness to both genders, we alternate the use of "he" and "she" among the books.

Printed on recycled paper in the United States of America

Contents

> "Attitude,
> not aptitude,
> determines
> altitude!"
> —Richard Weaver

The Three Keys to Good Self-Esteem

Self-esteem is the confidence you have in your abilities, the satisfaction you take in your accomplishments, and the respect you have for yourself. It is the result of an inner sense of success, satisfaction and optimism.

Good self-esteem occurs when an individual feels worthwhile and competent, when he believes that he belongs, is valued and liked. It is rooted in childhood experiences of love, support, acceptance and approval.

Good self-esteem is rooted in childhood experiences of love, support, acceptance and approval.

Self-esteem grows out of three key elements:

- acceptance
- competence
- purpose

A change in any one of these elements can have an affect on the others. For example, if your child develops competence in a sport, that competence may promote acceptance by classmates. Even though schoolwork will still be difficult, your child may feel better about going to school. The reverse is also true. A negative change in one of these three elements, for instance, can adversely affect the other two.

Acceptance is a sense of belonging. It is the security of knowing you are part of a family or group. Acceptance is also assuredness, feeling comfortable and safe, and being able to depend on individuals and situations. Outside the home it comes from inclusion, support, recognition and respect. Inside the home it comes from love, trust, appreciation, protection and encouragement.

Acceptance is a sense of belonging...the security of knowing you are part of a family or group.

Acceptance is demonstrated at home by:

- assuring your child that you love him, even when he's having problems

- providing a supportive structure, clear limits and consistent rules

- complimenting your child frequently and correcting her infrequently

- directing correction at your child's behavior, not at him ("Drawing on the wall is bad" not "You are bad")

- providing opportunities for your child to succeed and celebrating her successes

- supporting your child's efforts, inside the home and out

- encouraging friendships and helping your child develop social skills

Competence is the feeling of being able to handle the challenges you meet in life. It is knowing your strengths and understanding your limitations. It is having a feeling of success and accomplishment in the things you regard as

Competence is the feeling of being able to handle the challenges you meet in life.

important and valuable. The feeling of confidence is a very personal experience. A child caught in a pattern of putting herself down may not even have the skills to accept a compliment when she does a good job. To counter this lack of self-confidence, you can help by:

- giving your child respect and attention, even when she's not sure of herself
- encouraging areas or skills where your child has a strong interest
- supporting strengths and accepting weaknesses without dwelling on them
- helping your child recognize that her actions make a difference
- teaching your child to measure and appreciate his progress
  - pointing out things that your child does well
  - taking an interest in your child's activities

Purpose is having a clear vision of what you want, recognizing intentions, interests, wishes, dreams and, most importantly, goals.

Purpose is having a clear vision of what you want, recognizing intentions, interests, wishes, dreams and, most importantly, goals. Purpose is also an inner drive, a personal mission, a reason and motivation in life. When your child experiences failure at school, he may feel that his goals are unattainable and that nothing turns out right. You can help by:

- helping your child break down large objectives to create attainable goals
- promoting your child's goals and recognizing her accomplishments
- appreciating your child's efforts and telling him how well he is doing
- providing incentives and rewards to recognize your child's progress
- viewing your child's successes as permanent and personal

When you focus on your child's strengths, your child will do the same.

- helping your child recognize that there is always a way around a barrier

- expressing a positive attitude about your child's abilities and promise for the future

Your child needs good self-esteem to successfully cope with reading problems, now and throughout life. Believing in your child and loving him are the first steps to helping him gain a positive image of himself. When you focus on your child's strengths, your child will do the same.

Understanding the Difference Between Reading and Learning

It is important not to confuse the inability to read with the inability to learn. Confusing the two may lead some to conclude that children who cannot read are "slow" or "dumb." For many children, low self-esteem starts with this misunderstanding.

Reading is an acquired skill, like typing, riding a bicycle, playing an instrument or doing arithmetic. Learning is the process of getting information, remembering it and using it.

If reading is hard for your child, you need to help her find other ways to get information. (See *Step 4: Helping Children Read and Learn.*) She can learn to be skilled at watching, listening, asking questions and talking to other people. If your child reads poorly, she can learn from oral reading, group discussions, teacher explanations, activities, projects, audio and video tapes, films, and even talking computers.

Poor reading can be a serious problem, but it does not have to keep your child from learning. There are many ways you can help her develop alternative learning skills. You know your child better than anyone. You know what motivates and frustrates her. You have a powerful opportunity to nurture the skills, interests and desires that will support her success in school and beyond.

Turning the Spotlight on Your Child's Strengths

It is easy to understand how a child with a reading problem can develop a poor self-image. Research shows that 70 percent of what teachers and parents say to children is critical to their self-esteem. To balance the tendency to focus attention on correcting problems at school, take time to recognize your child's strengths and talents. Then encourage your child's unique abilities, value them, and watch your child grow.

Research shows that 70 percent of what teachers and parents say to children is critical to their self-esteem.

Here are some steps to get you started:

1. **List your child's strengths and interests**
   Make a list of your child's strengths and abilities. Ask your child to create a list, too. Then compare your lists and add them together. You may also want to ask others— friends, teachers, scout leaders, grandparents—to make their own lists of your child's good points. People who see your child in different circumstances or from different points of view (as a guest, for instance, or in the classroom, or in a large group), may see strengths you both may be surprised to discover!

2. **Accentuate the positive**
   Be specific when you praise your child, and focus on the positive.

   • Acknowledge gains in achievement: "You've really improved your grades. Good work!"

   • Acknowledge motivation: "I really appreciate that you set the table without being asked."

- Focus on what went right, not what went wrong: "Wow! You got seven of these spelling words correct!"

- Show appreciation for good actions and intentions: "Thank you. You're a big help to me."

- Frequently catch your child doing something right: "That was nice of you to fix your brother's broken toy."

3. Praise your child often, and teach him how to accept compliments

A child with low self-esteem not only thinks poorly of himself, he may also assume other people think poorly of him. Help your child learn how to accept success. Compliment him often, and tell him it's okay to say "Thank you" when someone sincere says something nice to him.

4. Encourage outside interests

Supporting your child's interests in non-academic subjects is a great way to boost his ego even when things are not going well in the classroom. Give your child the opportunity to discover different activities and experience new things. The following organizations can help you begin:

- recreational centers such as the YMCA, YWCA or a local community center

- local library, school or after-school programs

- organizations for children, such as 4H groups and scouts

- museums that offer workshops devoted to children

- fine arts and performing arts departments of local colleges and universities

Help your child learn how to accept success.

For more ideas, look in the yellow pages of your phone book under **Youth and Children,** or watch the newspaper's local community section for information about appropriate groups or events.

You might also suggest that an older child volunteer with a nearby pet rescue group, nursing home or community center. By volunteering, your child can build confidence, develop social skills and experiment with new activities while feeling good about helping others.

All behaviors have a purpose. If a child misbehaves, he may be trying to feel accepted, or reassure himself that he belongs.

Understanding Inappropriate Behaviors

It is not easy for children who fail in school to understand and value their own strengths and abilities. When a child fails at reading, she may not be getting the information and knowledge that reading provides. Without access to written information, she may not be able to make intelligent contributions to discussions in class, or clearly express her thoughts and feelings.

A child who cannot do things as fast or as well as other children may conclude that she cannot succeed at anything. Her feelings of failure may lead her to question her right to belong to the group. Sometimes, other children add to the problem by taunting or rejecting the child with reading differences. Rejection and the natural desire that all people have to belong to a group may lead a child with learning problems to try inappropriate behaviors.

All behaviors have a purpose. If a child misbehaves, he may be trying to feel accepted, or reassure himself that he belongs. For example, a child might choose companions that his parents do not approve of, or he may spend time with children of different age groups, or with children who get in trouble with school or local authorities. He may choose these groups because he feels accepted by them, and rejected in other areas of life.

Another child might use poor behavior to get her parents to notice her and give her the attention she seeks. For some children, even negative attention is better than feeling a constant lack of attention. A child may also seek attention by behaving in a difficult manner. She might prolong a homework assignment, for instance, to extend the time she spends with her parents.

Problems are solved best when discussed rationally and logically, and not "in the heat of the moment."

Poor behavior can also be an avoidance tactic. Some children deliberately avoid situations that will contribute to their feelings of failure and isolation. For example, a child might cause trouble in school to ensure that he is removed from the classroom before he has to read out loud or take a test.

Once you have identified the reasons your child may be behaving improperly, talk with her about them. Communicate a set of rules to solve the problem and consistently apply them. Take the opportunity to  assess your child's feelings about herself and help her find acceptance in more positive ways. Acknowledge and reward her accomplishments and positive efforts.

Finding Ways to Solve Problems

Problems are solved best when discussed rationally and logically, and not "in the heat of the moment." If you or your child are angry or frustrated, you should both take a break for a few minutes—or even an hour if you need it—before coming back together to discuss a problematic situation.

Start small

Do not take on a huge task or try to solve everything at once. If there is a particularly large problem you want to work on with your child, break it into smaller pieces and work on them individually. For instance, if your child is late for everything, start by figuring out how she can make it to school on time, then to soccer practice on time, then to dinner, and continue on.

Work together

When solving problems with your child, try these simple steps:

1. Voice your concern

Parent: "I notice you've been spending all your time on sports lately. Your grades seem to be slipping."

Child: "Yeah. I'm not good at schoolwork, so why bother?"

2. Listen and do not argue

Parent: "Sometimes schoolwork is hard, I agree."

Child: "I don't see any sense in it. I keep trying and trying, but nothing I do ever goes right."

3. Acknowledge frustrations and come back to the problem

Parent: "I know it's hard, but it needs to get done, right?"

Child: "I guess so, but I don't like it."

Parent: "I know. What do you have to do to finish your work?"

Child: "I have a paper due next week, but I don't understand what I'm supposed to write about."

4. Discuss possible solutions; listen to your child's ideas and suggest your own

Parent: "Do you want to talk to your teacher about it tomorrow? I can take you in a little early. Or maybe you'd like to call Karen. She's in the your class, isn't she? Maybe she can help."

Child: "No, I don't want to talk to Mr. Milton. And Karen was absent last week."

5. Decide on a plan of action and encourage positive steps

Parent: "Who else can help you get started?"

Child: "I don't know. I guess I can call Melissa."

Parent: "Good idea. Here's the phone. I'll make some popcorn for you while you're working. Let me know if I can help."

Write a Contract

When you come to an agreement with your child about the kind of work you expect from him, or a change in an inappropriate behavior, you may want to write it down in an agreement, or a "contract." With a contract, both you and your child can have a clear idea of goals and expectations.

Contracts should:

- be written at the child's level

- focus on one behavior at a time

- make the goals easily attainable

- offer reasonable rewards that your child will value

> **With a contract, both you and your child can have a clear idea of goals and expectations.**

For example, a contract might say:

> "I, Daniel, will complete all my homework for five nights in a row. When I accomplish this goal I can watch one extra hour of television on Saturday morning."
>
> _____
> **(Child's signature)**
>
> _____
> **(Parent's signature)**

Don't give up!

There may be other ways you can help support your child as she works. Use a time sheet or some other way to record time spent on homework. Offer her small, frequent rewards for sticking to her plan at first, and reduce the rewards as the plan becomes routine.

When you come up with a plan, check on it every day or two at first, and then less often later. This is an ongoing process. If it doesn't work out the first time, sit down with your child and try again.

Letters to School

Sometimes you can help your child succeed by sending short notes to his teacher, sharing information about goals, abilities and successes. If your child agrees, you might send his teacher a note like this one, which highlights how a special interest can tie in with a class project:

> Dear Mr. Tyler:
>
> Hector told me you are teaching about rainforests and how important it is to protect our environment. I thought you would like to know that one of Hector's hobbies is to make things out of clay, and he has begun to make a clay model of a rainforest. If Hector could bring his model in to school, it would boost his confidence and help him demonstrate what he is learning. Please let me know if this is a good idea, so that we can make arrangements.

If you want to write to the teacher to suggest ways your child could be helped in class, you might write a note like this one, which conveys acceptance of your child's difficulties and suggests one way to solve a problem:

> Dear Ms. Chen,
>
> As you know, my daughter Lisa has been working hard to learn American history, but she has difficulty with some of her reading skills. It might be helpful if she could do part of her classroom reading at home so she can keep up with the other students. Would it be possible to get information about upcoming reading assignments?

This note highlights a child's competence, and lets the teacher know you appreciate that he is being supported in class:

> Dear Ms. Johnson,
> Since we met last month, Jose has been able to complete his math homework without my pushing him. He is working independently, and seems pleased with what he is doing. Thanks for working with him!

This note asks for help from a teacher and indicates a child's intentions to learn, participate and succeed. A note like this can help a teacher appreciate a child's goals and support her as she works to succeed:

> Dear Mr. Brady,
> Shawna says her goal is to complete three books by the end of the term. Would you be able to suggest some books that she would be able to read and that she might like? Thank you for supporting her eagerness to learn.

Respect the trust that your child has in you and do not discuss information that would embarrass him. Be sure to ask your child how he feels about your communications with his teacher. Show him the note you plan to send, and modify any information that he finds objectionable. If there is resistance, listen to your child and trust his judgment.

Steps to Success

1. **Acknowledge the problem and isolate it**

   Feelings about a reading problem can color your child's attitudes about his competency in many areas. Acknowledge to your child that his disability is real, that you will do what you can to help, and that the problem is a life-long one. Make sure your child understands that reading isn't the only way to get information, and that he can learn and succeed despite having a learning difference.

2. **Find ways to accommodate the reading problem**

   Find strategies to help your child succeed in each subject. For instance, if reading is required to learn historical information, find out if your child can listen to information on tape, watch it on a video, or have the information read aloud to her. Make sure the teacher knows that the child is willing to learn, even if she needs to do it in a different way. Reading problems make success more difficult, but they do not prevent learning.

3. **Work toward better reading**

   You and your child may experience frustrations because of his reading problems. It is important to remember that, with proper instruction, time and effort, reading does improve. There are also reading strategies that your child can learn to help him better understand what he reads. (See *Step 4: Helping Children Read and Learn.*)

4. **Encourage your child's natural interests and successes**

   Look for areas or subjects in which your child has an interest and shows some success. Support those areas in school and use groups outside of school, such as scout groups, sports leagues and church groups, to build interest. Acknowledge the challenges that your child faces, but focus on her interests and abilities.

5. **Write contracts for achievable goals and reward successful behaviors**

   Frustration often blocks motivation, but you can provide incentives that will encourage your child to continue working on behavior that will lead to success and good self-esteem. Talk with your child about behaviors both of you would like to see improve. Help your child feel motivated and achieve success with short-term contracts that reasonably reward positive behaviors.

6. **Listen to your child**

   Listen to what your child has to say. Listen to him talk about his feelings of failure or discouragement. After listening, confront his negative statements by repeating critical comments in a noncritical way. For example, if your child says, "I never get anything right," you could reply by saying, "I don't agree. Why do you feel that way?" Be prepared to listen to your child's full explanation. Then give him concrete examples of why you know he can—and has—succeeded in many things. Point out the things he does well. Encourage him to remember his good points, even when he is feeling disappointed about a particular failure.

7. **Praise your child often**

   Your child's experiences with schoolwork help shape the way she feels about herself. Failures and uncertainty may tend to hold her back and make her feel bad about herself. Feelings of success and confidence can move your child ahead and encourage her efforts. If too much attention is focused on failure, your child may lose motivation and self-esteem. Give your child frequent, specific praise. Let her know she is a capable person. Acknowledge the difficulty of the tasks she undertakes. Make sure she knows that everyone makes mistakes, and that making mistakes is a natural part of any learning process.

8. **Show that you love and support your child**

   Take the time to show your child that you love him. Empathize with him about a bad experience; rejoice with him when something good happens. Tell him and show him often that you love him. Building self-esteem is a process that takes your long-term, continuous support. When you believe in your child, he will begin to believe in himself.

9. **Get help if you need it**

   For reasons that are often obscure, low self-esteem persists in some children despite their families' best efforts to support them. Discuss a persistent self-esteem problem with a counselor, psychologist, physician or trusted family advisor.

Frequently-Asked Questions

Q. What else can I do to improve my child's self-esteem?

A. Ask the school counselor or psychologist for suggestions. Seek outside help from your medical or spiritual advisor. Look for useful information and suggestions in self-help books in bookstores and at the library.

Q. Should I discuss my child's reading problem with her?

A. Yes. Pick a time when you both are free from distractions and there is little tension between you. Begin by asking how things are going or by sharing your concerns about a specific problem. Listen carefully and hear what your child is saying.

   Reassure your child that the reading problem is not her fault and that she will improve. Mention famous people who have had reading problems (See *Step 1: Understanding Reading Problems: Does Your Child Have One?* for an extensive list). Highlight your child's strengths or special interests. Talk about strategies that can help bypass the problem and improve reading skills. Keep your side of the conversation short. A few words on each area are enough.

Q. How can I think of strengths when my child is having so much trouble with schoolwork?

A. It is difficult to think positively when your child's schoolwork is suffering. Discuss your child's feelings of frustration with him. Point out progress, support the small steps forward, and make a life for your child outside of class and schoolwork. He needs to see success and approval, and you need to feel good about what you're doing to help him.

Q. What do I do if my child will not study or practice?

A. Discuss your concerns with your child at a time when you are not pushing her to study or practice. Listen to her response and do not reject it or argue the points. Use neutral comments like, "It's hard to practice every day, isn't it?" or "I know that sometimes you don't feel like studying."

  After listening for a while, try to work toward a contract that provides both short-term (daily) and long-term (every week or two) rewards. It is important to offer rewards that your child values and that you can reasonably provide. Once your child passes through difficult times, she will begin to value her newly-acquired skills and feel a sense of accomplishment.

Q. What do I do when my child's hobby is taking time away from his schoolwork?

A. Discuss your child's schedule during a peaceful moment. Voice your concerns and suggest that you work out a time schedule. Work together to draw up a chart showing the days and hours for each activity. Agree on reasonable, workable times for schoolwork and for his hobby. Arrange his schedule so that you are not required to remind him of his plans. If the new schedule is not working after several days, review the plan with your child and make necessary adjustments.

Resources

Articles/Internet Resources

Islands of Competence, by Dr. Robert Brooks, *LD Matters,* Winter 1997. Available from the Schwab Foundation for Learning, 1650 S. Amphlett Blvd. #300, San Mateo, CA 94402. 800-230-0988
Full text available at:
www.schwablearning.org

Stress Management for the Learning Disabled, by Ronald L. Rubenzer, Reston, VA: ERIC Clearinghouse on Handicapped and Gifted Children, *ERIC Digest #452.*
Full text available at:
www.cec.sped.org/digests/e452.htm

Talking to Children About Their Strengths and Weaknesses, by Dr. Mel Levine, *Parent Journal,* Autumn 1996. Available from the Schwab Foundation for Learning, 1650 S. Amphlett Blvd. #300, San Mateo, CA 94402. 800-230-0988
Full text available at:
www.schwablearning.org

Tips for Developing Healthy Self-Esteem In Your Child, developed by the Coordinated Campaign for Learning Disabilities.
Full text available at:
www.ldonline.org/ld_indepth/self_esteem/ ccld_tips.html

Self-Esteem Resources for Parents and Teachers

Look What You've Done! Learning Disabilities and Self Esteem (Video), presented by Dr. Robert Brooks, Washington, DC: PBS Video, 1997. Available from the publisher: 1320 Braddock Place, Alexandria, VA 22314-1698. 800-344-3337
http://shop.pbs.org

No One to Play With, by Betty B. Osman, Novato, CA: Academic Therapy, 1996.

Self-Esteem Revolutions In Children, by Thomas W. Phelan, Ph.D., Glen Ellyn, IL: Child Management Inc., 1996. Book and audio versions.

Understanding LD* Learning Differences: A Curriculum to Promote LD Awareness, Self-Esteem and Coping Skills in Students Ages 8-13, by Susan McMurchie and Pamela Espeland, Minneapolis, MN: Free Spirit, 1994.

When You Worry About the Child You Love: Emotional and Learning Problems in Children, by Edward Hallowell, New York, NY: Fireside, 1997.

Your Child's Self-Esteem, by Dorothy Corkill Briggs, New York, NY: Doubleday, 1975.

Self-Esteem Resources for Kids

Sometimes I Drive My Mom Crazy, but I Know She's Crazy About Me: A Self-esteem Book for Overactive and Impulsive Children, by Lawrence E. Shapiro, King of Prussia, PA: Center for Applied Psychology, 1993.

Stick Up For Yourself! Every Kid's Guide To Personal Power And Positive Self-Esteem, by Gershen Kaufman and Lev Raphael; edited by Pamela Espeland, Minneapolis, MN: Free Spirit, 1990.

Parenting Resources

Loving Your Child Is Not Enough: Positive Discipline That Works, by Nancy Samalin and Martha Moraghan Jablow, New York, NY: Penguin USA, 1997. Book and audio versions.

Parents Guide to Learning Disabilities, by Stephen B. McCarney, Columbia, MS: Hawthorne Educational Services, 1991.

Positive Discipline, by Jane Nelsen, New York, NY: Ballantine Books, 1987. Book and audio versions.

When The Chips Are Down… Strategies For Improving Children's Behavior: Learning Disabilities And Discipline, presented by Richard LaVoie, Washington, DC: PBS Video, 1997. Available from the publisher: 1320 Braddock Place, Alexandria, VA 22314-1698.
800-344-3337
http://shop.pbs.org

To obtain resources listed, or to find updated resources, visit the Schwab Foundation for Learning web site: **www.schwablearning.org**

Parent-Support Worksheet

All About Your Child

How well do you know your child? Sit down with him and ask him these questions—or create a list of your own. Encourage him to tell you about his likes and dislikes, his ideas and dreams. It could give you some new insights about how he sees himself, and some clues about how you can help him feel good about himself.

What is your favorite hobby?

_____

What is your favorite subject in school?

_____

What is your favorite book or story?

_____

What is your favorite music group or singer?

_____

What makes you feel better when you're sad?

_____

What world problem would you like to solve?

_____

What do you hate the most when it happens to you?

_____

What do you like the most when it happens to you?

_____

What do you like to do when you're with your friends?

_____

If you could change something at school, what would it be?

_____

If you could change something at home, what would it be?

_____

What would you buy if you had ten dollars?

_____

What would you buy if you had ten thousand dollars?

_____

What would you like to be when you grow up?

_____

What is your idea of a perfect day?

_____

What else would you like to tell me about yourself?

_____